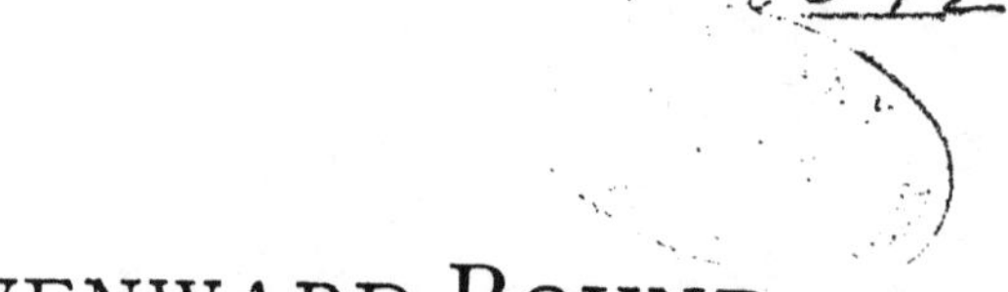

HEAVENWARD BOUND.

WORDS OF HELP FOR YOUNG CHRISTIANS.

BY

OLIVE A. WADSWORTH,

AUTHOR OF "BILL RIGGS, JR.," ETC. ETC.

A PRIZE BOOK.

PHILADELPHIA:

PRESBYTERIAN BOARD OF PUBLICATION,

1334 CHESTNUT STREET.

Westcott & Thomson,
Stereotypers, Philada.

"Christian saw a brave picture hang up against the wall, and this was the fashion of it: It had eyes lifted up to heaven, the best of books in his hand, the law of truth was written upon his lips, the world was behind his back; it stood as if it pleaded with men and a crown of gold did hang over its head."

A Prize of Two Hundred and Fifty Dollars, offered for the best book, of small size, for the instruction of young converts, was awarded to "HEAVENWARD BOUND."

CONTENTS.

CHAPTER VI.

CHAPTER VII.

CHAPTER VIII.

CHAPTER IX.

CHAPTER X.

CHAPTER XI.

CHAPTER XII.

PREFATORY.

I HAVE been asked to write a book of counsel for young Christians—something that might serve as a little light in a dark place, a little staff over a rough road, or a little sign-board pointing to the true way.

But writing is not like talking. Dear faces, bright eyes, responsive voices, draw out one's thoughts like so many magnets, while blank, emotionless paper seems to still them with its cold stare. And yet there are outside the reach of the voice so many more than within it, that one must even do at last as the apostle John did, when he desired greatly to see his dear ones face to face, but yet was compelled with pen and ink to write unto them.

And I am compelled; for necessity is laid upon me—yea, woe is unto me if I speak not loving words of gospel truth to young disciples. I love the *children* of the Lord, the younger brothers and sisters of our great family; they are the Josephs and Benjamins of our Israel, and my heart yearns over them, as Jacob's yearned over Joseph, and as Joseph's melted with tenderness for Benjamin.

Beloved young friends, let me indulge the fancy that I can see your earnest eyes turned toward me, and, for yourselves, take my words as lovingly as they are spoken.

Conversion.

“*The wind bloweth where it listeth, and thou hearest the sound thereof, but canst not tell whence it cometh, and whither it goeth: so is every one that is born of the Spirit.*”—JOHN iii. 8.

HEAVENWARD BOUND.

CHAPTER I.

Conversion of the Soul.

TO enter upon the discussion of duties and employments belonging to the Christian life, without first speaking of the turning of the soul from death to that life, seems hardly rational: it is like passing over the first round of the ladder by which we ascend, and trying to begin with the second. It is this very turning of the soul itself, this wonderful change in its nature, which demands and introduces new habits of thought, purpose and action, and it is well to inquire what this change is and how it comes about.

The simplest meaning of the word conversion is the "turning or changing from one state or condition to another, and in its full application does not refer merely to a person's speculative belief, but covers the whole tenor of his feelings and source of action." This may refer to a person's turning from one political or social condition to another; but where we apply the word to a religious process, we need a further and more definite explanation. What is this alteration that we must undergo? what is it to come into the kingdom of God? what is it to be converted? are among the first queries that arise in a thoughtful mind.

Many times in different forms has the question been asked me. Sometimes by children, whose little hearts longed to be changed before they even understood the process. Sometimes by the very ignorant, fearing in their darkness and humility lest they should fall into error. Sometimes by anxious, intelligent minds, sincerely desiring to understand, and yet bewildered and almost misled by the technical phrases of theologians. Sometimes by the petulant, half-interested, half-skeptical reasoner, who repudiates what he calls "dogmas and formulas," and demands the kernel of the matter in plain English that simple minds can easily grasp. Laying aside then all doctrinal phrases and every metaphysical or theological form of expression, we will look simply and candidly at the word of God. The Scriptures teach us that the conversion of the soul is a process in three parts: first, there must be a sense of want in ourselves—a conviction of our deep need of salvation; secondly, there must be an absolute belief that Jesus the Son of God is the one true and only Saviour, and holds the remedy we need; thirdly, there must be a solemn giving of ourselves to him, and an accepting of him in return as our Redeemer. We may discuss the matter, vary it, expatiate upon it as we will, but it all returns at last to these three simple propositions.

Let the feeling of our need come in whatever way it may—through sickness, through bereavement, through the gradual perception of God's mighty love, through the faithful preaching of the gospel, or the winning voice of the Holy Spirit in our heart—it must assuredly first come before we can heartily desire the help, the strength and the cleansing that only Christ can give. Many go as far as this point, and stop. They know they want something beyond themselves—something higher, better, more satisfying; they need something to supply their deficiencies, and lift them up into harmony with their Maker, and through ignorance or willful blindness they turn to every source but the right one. They put themselves in bondage to forms and ceremonies, and fast and use long prayers, or they force themselves to a rigid performance of external duties and occupations, or they seek relief in intellectual stimulants, in social enjoyments, or perhaps in still lower pursuits. Like the prodigal of old, they try to fill themselves with food only fit for inferior natures, instead of going direct to their Father's house; they seek to appease their craving with husks, while all the time He who alone can satisfy the hunger of the immortal soul—He who said of himself in those wonderful, deep-meaning words, "I am the bread of life"—stands by with patient tenderness, waiting to give them of that bread and of the water of life freely.

Others still, who feel their need of salvation and reverence Christ as the Redeemer of the world, stop short here and go no further. They neither expect nor hope for safety outside of him; they probably mean some day to take the last step that seals their safety, and accept him personally as their Saviour: in the mean time, they are *almost* Christians, but not quite. Are there not many such scattered through the households of our land, and worshiping in our churches on the Sabbath?—lovely, pleasant, honorable men and women, who verily are *not far* from the kingdom of God, and yet are not in it. When the last day comes, it will, alas, be found too late, that not to be with Christ is to be against him; that to be only *almost* in the kingdom of heaven is to be shut out of it for ever.

When the third and final step is taken, when the soul is given to God, its powers consecrated to his service, and his appointed plan of salvation through Christ personally accepted, the process is complete, and in common parlance conversion has taken place.

The Spirit of God seems to work in almost as many ways as there are individual Christians, and none should doubt the genuineness of the change in themselves, simply because its record cannot be made to tally with that of others. A great many most earnest and faithful disciples find it impossible to tell even when the change was going on within them; while others can point directly to a certain event, and say, "That sermon, or that prayer, or that dispensation of Providence, was the apparent means of bringing me to God." From the flower of grace, opening in tender baby hearts, to the palm of victory, won after life-long conflict by aged, trembling hands, there is every possible variety and phase of conversion.

A lovely old lady said once, regarding one of her daughters, who was a most devotedly pious person, that she could never remember the time when she was not a Christian. "I am sure," she said, "she was converted before she could talk. She was not only a Christian child, but a Christian baby, and her first broken lispings showed a tender little conscience and a heart full of love to God and man."

In the other extreme is a confession, listened to a few days ago by the side of a dying bed, where poverty, ignorance, age and mortal disease combined to oppress the sufferer. "It has been a long, dark struggle," she said. "I have been feeling for the light *so* long! For more than twenty years I've had little thoughts about God in my heart; little thoughts about his being very good and caring even for me; little thoughts about how I would like to know him better, and try to love him and please him. But there was no one to tell me how, no one to help, and I've been almost tired waiting! And now he himself has made it all plain. Jesus has shown me the way; he has put me in it; it takes me to him!" And the wan lips smiled, and the faded face shone with the peace of God.

If we recall a few of the conversions recorded in Scripture, their wonderful variety of manner manifests itself at once. Paul was changed almost instantaneously by a miraculous appearance—a heavenly vision of the very Jesus whom he was persecuting.

Timothy knew the Scriptures from a child, and was a thoroughly well drilled little Bible scholar, with mother Eunice and grandmother Lois always ready to teach him and talk with him. Lydia's heart the Lord opened, and with a gentle readiness she attended unto the things spoken by Paul. The jailer believed with fear and trembling, and Cornelius, that devout man, feared God, gave alms, and prayed always, for many years before the Holy Spirit was sent to him and his knowledge of the way of life was made perfect.

So we see there may be many methods of conversion, but the same spirit working in all; many ways of receiving the truth, but the same truth accepted by all; many divers circumstances surrounding the soul in its onward journey, but the same faithful Saviour receiving it at the end of its pil grimage.

We sometimes hear those who aim to be liberal rather than spiritual speaking of what they call the narrow views of Christians, "as if," they say, "no one could get to the truth except in just their way." In fact, it is but a few days since I overheard two persons sitting behind me in the cars talking together upon that very subject. "I believe there are more ways than *one* of getting to heaven," said one of them. "I do not believe salvation is shut up in this Church or that Church or any Church. No creed that ever was made will take a man there. Bigoted people may talk as they like, but I've no patience with such narrow-minded prejudice! There are more ways than one of getting to heaven!"

He spoke not only strongly, but bitterly, and I pitied him. For if there were so many ways, and he knew them, why could he not quietly take the one that suited him best without feeling bitter toward those who were inoffensively taking another? But the tones of his voice showed that he was fighting against his conscience; he was kicking against the pricks, and it was hard for him as it was for Saul. So I listened and pitied him in silence. We were just then approaching a junction, where several other lines of railway crossed our own at different angles, and as we stood waiting for another train to pass, I ran my eyes along the narrow iron ways as far as I could see. Upon one side they converged more and more closely as they approached their common termination, the great city we had left behind us. On the other they diverged rapidly, one crossing a distant river that was but just within sight; another following its course through level green meadows; a third, far away from either, stretching on, up between the hills and old gray rocks. My fancy wandered on beyond the limits of sight, and carried me along those level rails, through cities, villages, farm lands and forests, over wide prairies, through rocky passes and along flat, sandy deserts. Everywhere the same strong, even, well-laid, narrow way;

without it the best-constructed engine could make no progress, and could only be a panting, struggling, helpless thing, full of unused power, and utterly failing of its end. But give it the narrow track, which alone can serve its purpose, and its progress is assured. It passes indifferently through forest solitudes or the din of cities, through all climates, all soils, all scenes, in summer and winter, by day and by night, and safely reaches its destination at last.

It is but a homely illustration—and yet at that moment it seemed to my mind a forcible one—of the progress of the soul toward heaven. There is in truth but one way—one narrow way—that leads it thither; its course may run through widely varied scenes, through any nation or clime or Church, through joy or sorrow, health or sickness, wealth or poverty, but the way by which it journeys is Christ alone, and the end to which it tends is that blessed home above, prepared by him for those who love him.

So long then as we feel that Christ is indeed to our souls the way, the truth and the life, we need be troubled about nothing in the manner of our conversion, but rather strive to perfect the work of grace begun in us by every means that God has given, remembering his promise, that "he that shall *endure unto the end* shall be saved."

The story is told of a young man that soon after his conversion he confided the account of his spiritual experiences to his mother, and, having listened with deep interest, she answered in return: "All Christian graces may be counterfeited. Your love may be only a selfish love; your faith may be the faith that trembles; your hope and joy may be without a true foundation; but do not be discouraged, for there is one grace you can never counterfeit." "What is that, mother?" he asked. "The grace of perseverance," she replied.

To *continue* in well-doing is the thing that most concerns us. The past we have nothing more to do with; it has slipped completely out of our hands; and for the future, who shall boast himself of the morrow? But the present, the living present, the wonderful *now*, which God has called the accepted time, is ours. Let us use it with faithful diligence, going on from hour to hour as he shall lead us, forgetting that which is behind, and pressing toward that which is before, bearing ever in mind the words which Jesus spoke to those which believed on him: "If ye *continue* in my word, then are ye my disciples indeed."

Growth in the Soul.

"Like a tree planted by the rivers of water, that bringeth forth his fruit in his season."—Ps. i. 3.

CHAPTER II.

Growth in the Soul.

ONE of the most essential elements of Christian life is growth; or, to speak more accurately, it is a vital necessity, for without it there can be no true life, either physical, mental or spiritual. Wherever we look in the world of nature, we see expansion, accretion and development; and when a living thing ceases to grow, it begins to die.

In a plant, the dew, the rain, the sun, the tiny atoms of varied nutriment which are incessantly sucked from the ground by its rootlets, all tend to nourish it; the stalk pushes up, the leaves unfold, the buds swell, the flowers expand, the seed-vessel forms, the seeds mature, and, its full end being accomplished, the plant stops growing and withers slowly away. In a child the expansion of bone and muscle, the increase in height, breadth and weight, goes on often with astonishing rapidity, and when the body has attained its full size, the youth has, in popular language, finished growing. But does he in reality stop here? No; for now, as much as ever, does he need constant supplies of wholesome food to repair the continual waste that is going on within him. Play-days are over, and the work of life begins. The body toils, and in its daily action loses just so much actual strength and substance, which must be reinforced; the brain spends itself, and must be replenished. The hours of labor grow longer and longer, the period of rest shorter, and, even in that time of repose, the same work of change and growth goes on. The food which is eaten is divided by the process of digestion into good and bad, and while one is discarded as worthless, the other is taken into the blood and carried with its ceaseless current to every minutest portion of the body to reimburse its constant expenditure.

A very clever French physiologist, Jean Macé,* tells us that a man in health eats three times his own weight in the course of a year, and that the greater part of all this nutriment goes to supply the daily waste of flesh and tissue. The fire must have fuel, or it cannot burn, and when there is nothing more to feed the flame, it dies out. Hugh Miller, in one of his books, speaks of his writings in a tone of pleasantry as being the parings or shavings of his brain, and the expression is almost literally, as well as figuratively, true.

The immutable law of growth is just as absolute, though less perceptible, in spiritual things. Our Saviour compares the growing of grace in the heart to that of the corn in the field: first the blade, then the ear, then the full corn in the ear. In the beginning

* Author of a charming book for young readers, entitled "A Mouthful of Bread, and its Effect on Man."

it is a tender plant, sometimes as tiny as the grain of mustard-seed, which yet often develops into such size and strength that the fowls of the air lodge in its branches.

If our souls are to grow in spiritual things, we must give them all the essential conditions of growth: first, by setting them free from everything that can check their development; and secondly, by exposing them to every favoring influence that can foster it.

As we would pluck away the weeds that threatened to choke a dainty flower, so must we cast away every hindrance to spiritual advancement. If there be an evil passion, however knit into our characters; a hurtful companion, however dear; a noxious amusement, however fascinating; a self-indulgence that has become a part of ourselves; a folly, a vanity, a weakness, anything, no matter what, that bars the soul in its progress;—let it be thrust away without one murmur or one regret. "If thine eye offend thee (that is, cause thee to err), pluck it out," says the divine Word. "Nearer, my God, to thee, nearer to thee," is the longing of every loving heart, and that which brings it nearer is a willing sacrifice. It is only like throwing over the surplus lading of a ship, which may be worth something in itself, but which becomes valueless when it weighs the vessel down and stays or endangers its onward course.

Secondly, let us open our hearts wide, and invite all those influences and exercises which God has provided as a means of progress. These divide themselves naturally into two classes—those which relate to our inner life, and those which belong more especially to our external life.

In the former, which might almost be called the private life of the soul, we comprise faithful daily prayer and Bible-reading, the stated services of the church to which we belong, religious conversation, meditation upon holy things, and the cultivation of a meek and Christ-like spirit. For the outer life there must be the steadfast fulfillment of every duty belonging to the sphere in which God has placed us, helpful, cheerful ways to those around us, the active exercise of Christian benevolence according to our opportunity, and the upholding and encouraging of every good work going on about us, to the utmost extent of our ability.

Then, when we have done what we can, we may rest assured that God will do his share. He pours out his spirit in answer to our prayers; he opens our eyes to behold wondrous things out of his law. When those who love the Lord speak often one to another of him, he hearkens, and a book of remembrance is written before him for them that think upon his name.* And for help in all external acts of Christian beneficence or usefulness, he has given us these blessed words of encouragement: "Inasmuch as

* Malachi iii. 16.

ye have done it unto the least of these my brethren, ye have done it unto me."

But while we earnestly desire to grow, we must be careful that the process is equable, so that we may finally attain unto the perfect man, "the stature of the fullness of Christ."

It is a pitiable thing to be a one-sided, crotchety Christian, developed morbidly in some directions, and defective or totally lacking in others; yet we often see persons whose religious character has suffered such a twist, such an ungainly curvature, as almost to merit the name of a spiritual malformation.

The foolish mother among the Flathead Indians, who lashes a piece of wood to her baby's soft, little, immature head, cannot prevent the growth of the bones which compose it; she can only repress it in a certain direction, and Nature avenges the wrong by extending it in others, and so producing, by the period of maturity, a hideously flattened and imbecile-looking head. And in China, the babies of respectable rank pay for the advantage of good birth by having their compressible, little, high-born feet forced into the tiniest possible compass by torturing ligatures. They endure years of suffering before the end is accomplished. When the tight bandages are taken off, instead of a comely, elastic foot, surmounted by a shapely ankle, there is only a miserable, rudimentary little paw overhung by a monstrous mass of fat. All that should have gone to nourish and expand the foot being excluded from it took refuge naturally in the ankle, and both are deformed.

We are so much the creatures of sight and sense that while we pity and regret deformity of the body, we sometimes come nigh forgetting the vastly greater import of the crooks and twists of the moral nature. But if we open our eyes only to a part of God's dealings and shut them to others; if we open our ears to part of his teachings and deafen them to others; if we fasten our faith to any external form, to the opinions of man or to any earthly standard whatever; we certainly are binding about our souls a ligature that will inevitably repress spiritual growth in one way or another.

Sometimes people dwell upon and brood over one portion of God's word, for instance, till they can scarcely see any other. It is not long since I met a conscientious woman, whose belief in the overruling hand of God was so great that it had become the dominant idea of her life; it swallowed up everything else, and she had come to think of it almost as the Turks think of their "kismet"—the fate that comes inevitably upon them, do what they will. In circumstances that demanded the utmost vigilance and labor, the most prompt and energetic action, she would actually do nothing. "The Lord's will must be done," she said, "and we have only to wait."

Now we know there are times in God's

dealings with us when we can do nothing but wait—when he himself so ties and fetters us that our part seems simply to acquiesce in what he does; and thousands of patient hearts have throbbed in submissive sympathy with the last line of Milton's sonnet upon his blindness:

> "They also serve who only stand and wait."

But we may be sure, if God meant us *always* to "stand and wait," he would never have said to us, "Strive, watch, work, pray, feed the hungry, clothe the naked, visit the sick, preach the gospel."

There are others—who are surely very unhappy Christians—who seem to have lost sight of the wonderful tenderness and love of the almighty Father through the constant consideration of his attributes as Creator, Sovereign and Judge. They cherish terrible views of an offended and avenging God, forgetting the pitying kindness that shines through all his dealings with us, and that he is, in fact, a Father reconciled to us through Christ our Lord. It is a fearful thing so to misjudge God's great heart of love. "Thou knewest I was an austere man," are the solemn words of condemnation in the parable, "and out of thine own mouth will I judge thee."

Many other Christians bind themselves to some external mode of service or to a rigid routine of formal duty; but Mr. Legality, in the "Pilgrim's Progress," did not suffer one-half as much in his bondage as they in theirs; for he was but a hypocrite, while they are conscientiously holding fast to the very impediments which check the growth they truly desire.

We see, therefore, that many beliefs and practices, right and scriptural in themselves, may lead us into error when dwelt upon to the exclusion of others and separated from the whole word of God, which in its entirety is so admirably adapted to meet every want of the immortal soul. "All

Scripture is given by inspiration of God, and is profitable for doctrine, for reproof, for correction, for instruction in righteousness, that the man of God may be perfect, thoroughly furnished unto all good works." "These things ought ye to have done," said Jesus, "and not to leave the others undone."

And now, to secure this free development of a full Christian life, this thorough furnishing unto all good works, what shall we do and what shall we avoid doing? It is evident that the less dependence we place upon outward things—whatever they may be, whether forms of service, rules of action, the opinions of men or human models of excellence—and the nearer we draw to Christ, the higher and holier, the fuller and more perfect, our lives will be. The more directly we stand in the rays of the sun, the stronger the light and warmth we receive; the nearer we go to the fountain-head, the purer the water we quaff. The closer we draw to Christ, our great Sun and Fountain of life, the more fully we receive of his grace, his purity, his love, his all-sufficing righteousness.

He himself has given us the secret of growth—of free, rapid, healthy, satisfying growth—in three little words, "*Abide in me.*" "As the branch cannot bear fruit of itself, except it abide in the vine, no more can ye, except ye abide in me. I am the Vine, ye are the branches. He that abideth in me, and I in him, the same bringeth forth much fruit, for without me ye can do nothing."

To abide in Him now is to abide in him for ever, for the choice of Christ as our rest and our abode extends through time into eternity. If we would be like him upon earth, and live with him hereafter, let his solemn, loving, all-embracing words be indelibly engraven upon our willing hearts: "*Abide in me.*"

The Standard of Attainment.

"*As obedient children, not fashioning yourselves according to the former lusts in your ignorance; but as He which hath called you is holy, so be ye holy in all manner of conversation; because it is written, Be ye holy, for I am holy.*"—1 PET. i. 14–16.

CHAPTER III.

The Standard of Attainment.

IT is necessary for the rational pursuit of any object to have a definite end in view, toward which our efforts point and in which they are finally to culminate. The architect aims at the substantial and tasteful construction of a building; the farmer concentrates his efforts on securing a certain crop at a given time; the mariner uses his best skill to bring a valuable cargo safely to a destined port; the general bends every energy to achieve victory for his troops. Aimless building, farming, sailing and marching would ensure such absurd results as to merit a place of honor in the world of chance that Hafet dreamed of. As in worldly things a definite aim is necessary to induce the vigorous, well-directed, patient labor which alone can secure success, so in spiritual things it is as much more important as the worth of the soul outweighs that of the body.

The remark is often made by religious writers and speakers of the present day that the prevailing standard of personal religion among Christians is far below what it ought to be; and the truth of the observation may be easily proved by looking a little at our neighbors and still more at ourselves. As a nation, as congregations, as families, as individuals, how much less holy, wise and Christ-like are we than we ought to be!

Not only do religious writers speak of it with regret, but those who are pleased to find cause of reproach in the state of the Church comment on it without reserve. We give the enemies of the truth a vantage-ground that they do not fail to occupy. Some time ago—in one of the British reviews, I think—there was a satirical remark by a very clever but irreligious writer which struck me as being not wholly unmerited. He divides all Christians into three great classes—the Attitudinarians, the Latitudinarians and the Platitudinarians. We may evade the first charge by deeming the moral to be pointed more particularly at those of our fellow-Christians who belong to churches where the forms and ceremonies may sometimes devour the substance, as the lean kine devoured the fat kine; and the external rites—the outside, the *attitude*, in short—become pre-eminent.

And the second charge we may succeed in shifting upon the accommodating shoulders of our "liberal" friends upon the other flank, who love broad views and an unbounded creed.

But when it comes to the third charge, how many among us would dare to stand boldly up and plead "Not guilty!" For my own part, I can only hope that God will forgive us for making our religion and his service such a dull, flat, commonplace thing as we often do.

God has commanded us to love him not only with all our *heart*, but with all our *mind;* he united the intellectual faculties with the moral affections, and what God joined together men are continually putting asunder. Although there has been a great change of sentiment on this subject within a few years, we need vast improvement still. We are too apt to think that if a hymn, for instance, is pious, it need not be poetical; if a sermon is scriptural, it may be as dull as the American Annals; if a book is orthodox, it may be wretched in style and stupid in substance; when the fact is that hymn and sermon and book, or whatever else we do or say for God's glory or the good of men, should receive all the knowledge, the quickness, the wit, the talent and the time that we can give to it. It is not enough that a thing is good simply in a pious sense; the better it is in that way, the worse the fault in us to let it be deficient in other ways.

A very successful young minister once said to me that there had been a strange omission in his training as a preacher. "In all the teaching of my theological course," he said; "in all the sermons I have listened to on that subject; in all the advice I have had from older ministers,—I have received almost every imaginable counsel: I have been entreated to be orthodox, to be scriptural, to be simple, to be practical, to be personal; but nobody ever enjoined it upon me to be *interesting*—and what good can all the rest do without it? If you cannot interest your hearers, your words fall to the ground." He had learned the secret, however, as almost every preacher or teacher does learn it whose heart is bent on doing good to the utmost of his power.

God certainly helps those who look to him not only to be good, but to be wise, to attract others, to draw hearts and win souls;

and I believe it lies within our power not only to preach better sermons and write better books, but also to infuse far greater vitality, warmth and interest into the simple daily life of the soul. We are told not to despise the day of small things, but we are nowhere bidden to be *satisfied* with it; but rather to press forward, to shine more and more, to go from strength to strength, and to be content only when we are perfect as *He* is perfect.

If we look at some of the causes which have tended to lower the standard of Christian life among us, it may help us the better to apply the remedies. In our own country we see very plainly that a species of religious insubordination, if it may be so called, has arisen as a direct reaction from the extreme rigor that was exercised in such matters a century or more ago.

One extreme invariably produces another. The exiles who sought in the wilderness of America to secure for themselves and their children a home, where they might establish a "Church without a bishop and a State without a king," were themselves in a state of reaction from the reckless, godless license of that Church and State from which they were escaping.

The rebound from lawlessness was into too much law. The recoil from unprincipled levity was into a rigid austerity; and men noble, pure and sincere beyond reproach, were led by the overstrained condition of heart and brain into an unwise severity of dress, speech and manner—into harshness of private discipline and public government.

We smile now at the angularity of some of their rules of action and at the laws framed in those days, yet we ourselves may learn a lesson from them—a lesson that the world has been long in acquiring—namely, that consciences must be *guided*, not forced; *led*, and not driven. There are cases where we are compelled to make such rules, because children and inferiors have not enough judgment or experience to enable them to live without them; but in all instances the sooner true principles of right and wrong can be instilled into their hearts, and a consciousness of individual responsibility to God established, the sooner rules may be discarded and the happier and better for all concerned.

Principles are like the ever-ascending sap in a young tree—an incessantly active, vital power that penetrates to every tiny leaf and twig and urges it to healthy growth. *Rules* are like the firm-set stake to which we tie the sapling to keep it upright in its tender years. If we imagine a rather independent young tree, quite disdaining its external prop, feeling that the time has come when it can stand alone, and, in its haste to be free, bending so far away from the stake as to acquire a decided curve in the opposite direction, we shall have a figure of the way in which it seems to me that some of the rigidity and sternness of our forefathers are showing their reactive effects in the easy, liberal, too careless views of many Christians of the present day.

There is another reason spoken of by Dr. Goulburn in his excellent "Thoughts" on this subject, which applies to the standard of religion in all Christian countries.*

"Is it not the case," he says, "that there is a singular analogy between the present state of knowledge and of piety; that in this age literature and religion fare much alike? In what were called the Dark Ages, literature was the monopoly of the few; gross ignorance was the condition of the many. It is not so any longer. Every one knows a little; few know much. Is it not the same with piety? The great saints of

* "Thoughts on Personal Religion," by E. M. Goulburn, D.D. The writer of this admirable book, being a clergyman of the Church of England, has some views incident to his position (especially as regards Communion and Confirmation) which, of course, are not in unison with our own; otherwise his teachings are most excellent.

primitive times stand out like stars in the firmament of the Church, all the brighter for the darkness of heathenism or of superstition which surrounds them. But the tendency of modern times has been to diffuse among many the piety which was once concentrated in the few. The public are religious as a public; but in individuals the salt has lost its savor. Everybody can speak volubly upon controversial subjects; but where are the men upon whose hearts the truth, which is at stake in controversies, is making every day by means of prayer and meditation a deeper imprint?

"Is there any flaw in our ministry which may in some measure account for the low standard of personal religion on which we have been commenting? We fear there is. We believe that the Christian ministry having, by God's design and constitution, two arms wherewith to do its work, one of these arms has become paralyzed by inactivity. We believe that its office being twofold—to rouse consciences and to guide them—we have for a long time past contented ourselves with rousing, while we have done scarcely anything to guide them. The impression has been that people know everything about Christian duty, and have no need to be enlightened on that head. And if by Christian duty be meant simply the moral law of God in its outward literal aspect, perhaps the impression is more or less correct, at least as regards the educated classes. But if by Christian duty be meant sanctity of life and character and a growing conformity to the image of the Lord Jesus, we must be pardoned for expressing our conviction that our best and most respectable congregations have very little insight into the thing itself, and still less into the method of its attainment."

Dr. Goulburn's remarks recall the words of a very excellent minister on the subject of admitting young persons into the Church. "We cannot let them enter too early," he said, "if we only continue to guide and teach them; but the trouble is, we gather our lambs into the fold and then starve them. The good Shepherd, who called himself also the door of the sheep, said that all who entered in by him should be saved, and should *go in and out and find pasture.* But our poor lambs we leave to themselves, to feed or famish as they may. Let us feed the lambs, nourish them, sustain them, lead them, and then it matters not how young or ignorant they may be at first."

There is another cause still to be found for the low standard of personal religion in the facility of the Christian life in our days, its smoothness and lack of self-denial. The way is wide open, persecution has ceased, restrictions are removed and the world respects rather than despises a consistently religious man. Wisdom's ways are ways of pleasantness and all her paths are peace. Her warfare is within and not without, for her external foes are vanquished or changed to friends.

But it pleases me to think that, if necessity should arise, men would suffer and die for the name of Christ as unflinchingly now as in the days of the martyrs. When our civil war broke out a few years ago, taking us unawares, in the midst of peace, we were a quiet, busy people, given to trade, manufactures, arts and professions—as unwarlike, apparently as unfit for martial conflict, as a people could possibly be. But as soon as there became a necessity for action, for self-sacrifice and endurance of hardship, thousands of hearts awoke and responded to the call. The love of country and fealty to its laws kindled and burned at the first breath of insult; and our home-bred, soft-looking, easy-going civilians proved themselves capable of the patience, courage and firmness of veterans. Hardships, sickness, wounds and death they met without a murmur. The more immense the demand upon them, the more heroic and unflinching they became.

I believe it is the same thing with many Christians of the present day; they appear indifferent, apathetic and slothful, because there is no external opposition to rouse them into action; but if such a shock should ever come, they would prove themselves true soldiers of the cross. But, after all, what a strange apology is this to make for lukewarmness and inactivity! It is the same as saying that because God has made the way easy, we will love him less; because he has removed barriers, we will serve him slothfully; because his mercy has been so great, our devotion shall be diminished. Shall we thus actually tempt God to chasten us by our lethargy in time of prosperity? Rather let us endeavor to reach the highest standard of Christian holiness that God has set before us, and thank him daily that the path has been made so plain and so peaceful.

It is of vital importance to us to deter-mine what that standard is toward which we are to climb. The Scriptures present to us many examples of goodness worthy of imitation: Moses was meek; Job was patient; Solomon was wise; David was prayerful; Peter was zealous; John was loving. No better human models can probably be found, and yet, alas! the very virtue for which each was pre-eminently renowned failed to maintain itself consistently in times of trial. Moses beat the rock with his rod, broke the tables of stone and slew an Egyptian in anger. Job was long-enduring, but under severe and repeated trial his patience failed, and he cursed the day he was born. Solomon was wise, but what a pitiful lack of understanding he displayed in cleaving to the strange wives and strange gods that beguiled him from the truth! David prayed with true fervor, but that he did not always watch as well as pray is evident from his life. Peter's zeal was warm and sincere, yet he denied the very Master he loved so deeply. John was gentle, tender and loving, but, had not Jesus forbidden him, he would have commanded fire from heaven to destroy the Samaritan village that would not receive the Saviour.

Among men there is none righteous—no, not one. If there had been—if but one individual of our race could have fulfilled the law and satisfied the requirements of God—we should never have needed the vast sacrifice of the Son of God, who was offered to bear the sins of many and to fulfill all righteousness for us. There is no earthly model for us to imitate—no perfect example anywhere among the sons of men: he alone who bore pre-eminently the title of the Son of man, as well as that of the Son of God, can serve as our standard of true holiness.

No matter how far above us he may stand, we need not be discouraged by that, for he himself has promised to aid us. What succor, what refuge, could we find, were our Rock not higher than we? We can be *like* him in character, if not truly to the same degree; the same *mind* may be in us that is in him, though ours be feeble with mortal littleness, while his is great and bright with divine glory. A low aim gives but low results; let us therefore aspire to the highest and best; let the Christian watchword be Excelsior! climbing higher and higher, reaching upward and onward, leaving earthly things behind, and seeing for the pattern of our daily life no man, but Jesus only.

His mortal life spreads itself out before us as the one faultless, heaven-imprinted life on earth. His early days were full of obedience and gentleness, submission to the authority of home, a daily increase in wisdom and such lovely graces of mind and heart as won the favor of God and man. His maturity possessed an infinite patience, unfailing tenderness for the sick and sad, pity and beseeching words for the erring, free forgiveness for bitter enemies, ceaseless charity, loving deeds, vast self-denial, perfect beneficence, fervent prayer and radiant peace. But how can we speak of the character of Jesus in a sentence, in a chapter, or in a volume even?* Let us daily seek the record of his words and deeds in the Scriptures he has given us; and praying for full comprehension of their wondrous grace and fullness, by the help of the Spirit draw nearer and nearer to him, our perfect Example, knowing that if here on earth we can never reach the height for which we strive, he will at last lift us up unto himself, and we shall "be satisfied when we awake in his likeness."

* The beautiful chapter on this subject in Dr. Bushnell's "Nature and the Supernatural," is now published in a small volume by itself, called "The Character of Jesus."

Christian Life—Spiritual and Practical.

"*If ye love me, keep my commandments.*"—John xiv. 15.

62

CHAPTER IV.

Christian Life—Spiritual and Practical.

THE fully-developed life of a Christian is a twofold existence, whose diverse aspects are indicated in the words of our Saviour used above. There must be the emotions of the heart, beating with love to God, and the external action required in the keeping of his commandments. One is the inner, the other the outer life; one is the spiritual, the other the practical existence; one has its exponent in faith, the other in works; but however satisfactorily we may be able to divide the two in discussion, in reality they should always be united.

The receptive and meditative faculties are most used in all that pertains to the inner life, while that which concerns the outer employs the active and energetic qualities of the mind. The soul must first receive before it can give forth again; and in proportion as the spiritual life is deep, holy and fervent, the practical life will be faithful, fruitful and Christ-like.

There are, without doubt, some exceptions to this rule, as in the case of timid persons, whose faith is sincere, but weak, and who shrink from all outward assertion of allegiance to their Master; or, in that of less worthy individuals, whose love of activity, natural benevolence or desire to produce an impression of some kind induces them to engage in works of beneficence, without a trace of pure and holy prompting in the heart. Still, in the vast majority of cases the beauty and usefulness of the outer life maintain a direct relation to the progress of the life within. That soul which opens itself most willingly to God's teachings, which draws the closest to him and receives of his abundance, will surely give forth again its gifts in a lovely, faithful daily life and conversation.

Faith and works can never be disunited; they are like the figure eight, which, severed through the centre, makes only two worthless naughts, quite valueless by themselves. Faith without works is but a feeling, not a faith; and works without faith are only husks without the kernel, leaves without fruit. Abraham was faithful; he believed God, and it was imputed unto him for righteousness, but it was that true and living faith that proves itself by works. If he had said quite zealously, "Lord, I believe, but I cannot quite make up my mind to leave my own land and kindred; I believe, but it seems a little too hard to follow your call, I know not where; I believe, but I would rather keep Isaac,"—would this belief have been accounted to him for righteousness, and would he have won the honored name of "Faithful Abraham?" No; his works followed immediately upon his faith; they sprang with it, rather, from a heart consecrated to God.

In a number of cases Christ commended the faith of different persons who came to him for help, but when we examine them, we find in every instance, without exception, that the faith was accompanied with works; earnest effort, importunate pleading or offerings of devotion. The centurion, whose servant was sick, came out to meet Jesus beyond the city as he was approaching, and besought him to speak the word only, without coming under his unworthy roof. Blind Bartimeus cried after him for mercy, and when many bade him hold his peace, he called out the more vehemently, "Jesus, thou son of David, have mercy on me!" The woman who was a sinner followed him into Simon's house, a most unwelcome guest, stood by him as he sat at meat reclining in Eastern fashion, and bathed his feet with her tears, wiped them with her long hair and anointed them with costly ointment. The woman of Canaan followed him long, despite every obstacle; Jesus would not notice her, the disciples wanted to send her away, and when, at last, the Saviour spoke, it was to discourage her. Still she followed him, pleaded with him and worshiped him, till, at last, she received the boon she wanted and the blessed commendation, "O woman, great is thy faith!"

There are some verses in the second chapter of the Epistle of James which combine, perhaps better than any others in the Bible, the full relation between faith and works, and condense whole treatises into a few sentences: "What doth it profit, my brethren, though a man say he have faith, and have not works? Thou believest that there is one God; thou doest well; the devils also believe and tremble. But wilt thou know, O vain man, that faith without works is dead? Was not Abraham, our father, justified by works when he had offered Isaac, his son, upon the altar? Seest thou how faith wrought with his works, and by works was faith made perfect? Ye see, then, how that by works a man is justified, and not by faith only; for as the body without breath is dead, so faith without works is dead also."

Putting beside this the declaration of St. Paul to the Ephesians, that by grace we are "saved through faith, not of works, lest any man should boast," we come necessarily to the conclusion that in God's sight neither is complete without the other. Through the grace of God sinful men are provided with an all-sufficient Saviour; through faith they accept him for their own, and rest in his salvation; through works they prove the soundness and vitality of their faith, and honor him they call Master. What link can we spare from this very short, but strong, chain that binds us to Christ and his service?

Faith, without works, is indeed dead, the

Apostle James says, and works without faith are but a ghastly semblance of life. They are like the mechanical action of an automaton, or the galvanic movements of a dead body, simulating the motions of vitality, but impelled solely by external force and not by the promptings of the burning, breathing, informing spirit.

Mr. Spencer has used a forcible illustration in speaking of the relation which faith holds to the other Christian graces. "The root of a tree," he says, "is a ragged and jagged thing in shape, no proportion, no comeliness in it, and therefore keeps itself in the earth, as unwilling to be seen; yet all the beauty that is in the tree, the straightness of the bulk and body, the spreading fairness of the branches, the glory of the leaves and flowers, the commodity of the fruits, proceed from the root; by that the whole subsisteth. So faith may seem but a sorry grace, a virtue of no regard. Devotion is acceptable, for it honors God; charity is noble, for it does good to man; holiness is the image of heaven, therefore beauteous; thankfulness is the tune of angels, therefore melodious. But what is faith good for? Yes, it is good for every good purpose, the foundation and root of all graces. All the prayers made by devotion, all the good works done by charity, all the actual expressions of holiness, all the praises sounded forth by thankfulness, come from the root of faith, that is the life of them all. Faith doth animate works, as the body lives by the soul. Doubtless, faith hath saved some without works, but it was never read that works saved any without faith."

For the sake of simplicity, we have hitherto taken "faith" to stand for all the inner experiences of the Christian life, and "works" to represent its varied external manifestations. In pursuing the subject further, we must necessarily examine these two phases of religious life more in detail, and for that purpose must divide them, as they never should be divided in a true Christian experience, and consider them quite separately.

As the outer life depends upon the inner, lives by it, grows in proportion to its growth and decays with its decay, we will speak first of the things which belong to the spiritual life, its nourishment, its development, and subsequently of its final expression in those external acts which belong to the Christian's practical life.

Spiritual Life: Prayer Offered.

"*O Lord God of Israel, there is no God like thee in the heaven nor in the earth; which keepest covenant and shewest mercy unto thy servants, that walk before thee with all their hearts; then what prayer or what supplication soever shall be made of any man or of all thy people Israel—hear thou from heaven, thy dwelling-place, and forgive, and render unto every man according to all his ways, for thou only knowest the hearts of the children of men.*"—2 CHRON. vi. 14, 29, 30.

CHAPTER V.

Spiritual Life: Prayer Offered.

THERE are many words and phrases belonging to religious things, which have become so current among us, such frequent, every-day utterances, that our accustomed ears hear them almost mechanically, and their sound rarely rouses us to a consideration of the full meaning conveyed by them.

Of all such, the word prayer is one of the most remarkable, both for the frequency with which it is used and for the wonderful power, beauty and mystery which are comprehended in it, for it has been well said that "prayer moves the Arm that moves the world."

In considering its true nature, we choose

from its many aspects and phases three dominant ones, which may be made to comprehend all, or nearly all, the others. *First*, prayer as an act of homage, adoration and worship toward the almighty Maker of heaven and earth, the Creator, Preserver and Ruler of all. *Secondly*, prayer as a means of making known our wants and supplying our necessities, comprising all petitions for body and soul, confessions of sin and thanksgiving for blessings received. *Thirdly*, prayer as a medium of communion between the trusting, loving soul and the still more loving Saviour—a method of interchange, as it were, of deep, heartfelt devotion on the one side, and deeper peace and rest on the other.

True reverence and homage God has a right to demand from every creature upon earth. However proud, however great, however careless of their souls' eternal welfare, they may be, they owe allegiance to the great Author of all, as to the King who reigns, the Judge who arbitrates, the vast Power whose matchless intelligence controls, pervades, impels and perfects all. Natural religion, aside from all that is revealed, proclaims such wonders, from the vast systems of worlds maintained in absolute order and motion through the whole creation, down to the indescribably minute and perfect life revealed by the microscope, that it compels the deepest wonder, reverence and praise from every rational mind for the great Head and Source of all.

But in coming to God with our petitions, we need not so much to remember the grander attributes of his omnipotence as the more tender qualities of his fatherhood—his loving-kindness, his gentleness, his willingness to pardon, his readiness to use the vast resources of his eternal nature to help and bless and save his children.

"His love is as large as his power,
And neither knows measure nor end."

And both are for us, strange as it may seem. Human assertions could never make us believe it; the fact is so wonderful, so vast, our finite minds can scarcely grasp it; but we have God's own word for it, and so we must take it simply and fully, with grateful hearts, believing, as he says, that the feeblest prayer, the faintest, poorest cry for help, come up before the throne of his Majesty on high, and are heard and answered.

The third aspect of prayer which we have mentioned is perhaps the highest and holiest of all. It is not an act of homage, it is not an appeal for help. It is more a yearning for the presence of God, a happy hungering and thirsting of the soul after righteousness—happy because it knows it shall be filled; it is an opening of the whole heart to its Saviour in deep self-consecration, in absolute trust, in blessed consciousness of his unchanging love. It is an intense but peaceful longing to be like the beloved

Redeemer, to be with him, to abide in him, to be one with him. Most often it may be an inarticulate, wordless prayer, for with the heavenly Friend, as with an earthly, silence is often as sweet as converse; but the soul gives itself up to God's will, and is borne along on eagle's wings; it stays itself on Christ, and is kept in perfect peace.

A pagan, a worldling, or even a deist, may honor God as the Maker of the world, compelled by the wonder of his works in nature to reverence him as a higher Power. But his children approach him as a loving Father, and confidently ask for those things which he delights to bestow. And those who have experienced his deeper providences, and have received a further teaching of the Holy Spirit, have been brought to feel their own utter nothingness and the grace and fullness of Christ to such a degree as words can scarcely tell of. They have been shown the wonderful love which envelops them, leads them, succors them, gladdens them; which never leaves them nor forsakes them; which was set apart for them before the creation of the world, and is theirs for time and eternity. Then their highest joy on earth is to open their willing souls to the sunshine of that love and bask in it and be glad, as a little child in its mother's smiles.

When shall we pray? David says, "Evening, morning and at noon will I pray." Daniel went to his chamber and "kneeled upon his knees three times a day, and prayed and gave thanks to God." Whatever times we fix upon for our private devotions, and though they may vary in some cases through force of outer circumstances, the period most naturally accorded to such exercises will be morning and evening; whatever times we fix upon should be regular and stated times, as near the same hour every day and as nearly in the same place as possible. As regards our physical nature, we know that the food we eat daily, taken at certain regular hours, nourishes and sustains the body, while it becomes a bane almost more than a benefit, if eaten at odd times, with no regard to punctuality; the body not only misses its stated supply, but suffers from the irregular demands made upon it, and so derives comparatively little good from even wholesome food.

In spiritual matters it is very much the same. Irregular, almost haphazard prayer, offered one day at one time and another at another, can do little for us, compared with the good which follows the faithful use of a stated hour. We learn to put other things aside at that time, and those about us soon understand that they must leave us to ourselves; the same hour and the same place become associated in our minds with thoughts that are not of the world, and so help to bring us into a quiet frame.

But the prayer which is easily deferred for one thing or another—the prayer which waits for a leisure hour or a chance minute—

often waits all day and has lost the dew of the morning at last. The manna God gives us is both like and unlike that of the Israelites; like it, because we cannot accumulate it, but must gather it fresh day by day; unlike it and better, because theirs, "angels' food" though it was, lay scattered upon the ground and we gather ours directly out of God's own hand.

But shall we limit our prayers to one, two or three stated times a day? By so doing we shall often cut off our supplies when most needed. Ejaculatory prayer is as natural and involuntary to the child of God as the drawing of the breath. Sudden temptations take us, disappointment meets us, unkindness pains us, weariness overcomes us, and almost unconsciously our cry goes up to heaven for the escape, the solace, the repose that God stands ever ready to give. The more we accustom ourselves to the use of ejaculatory prayer the more help, strength and happiness shall we receive. To compare great things with small, it sometimes seems to me that our regular prayers are like the long letters we send to absent friends—minute, full and complete as epistles—while these little thoughts that fly to heaven and back with such rapidity are like the brief telegraphic messages we send them to ask a single question or state a single fact.

We must not, then, lose the great privilege which has been bestowed upon us, but avail ourselves of it, and in the words of the little mission-school card, "When tempted, when troubled, when sick, when afflicted, when oppressed, when forsaken, look to Jesus." But to me that little card has never been quite satisfactory. I should like to add to it, "When happy, when peaceful, when prosperous, when blessed, look up in joyous thanksgiving to Him who has given all."

How shall we pray? Not with high-sounding phrases and many words, which our Saviour calls "vain repetitions." "God is in heaven and thou on earth, therefore let thy words be few." Our reverence for God will naturally exclude careless and undignified expressions from our prayers, but let us be sure that it is the heart alone that God looks at. Beautifully written prayers undoubtedly please the writer and perhaps edify those who read them; and eloquent petitions, well delivered, probably satisfy the declaimer and suit the ears of the hearer; but the lisp of a trusting child or the heavenward sigh of an oppressed slave is as truly a prayer to God and more sure of an answer, for there is nothing in it but heartfelt need.

Let us remember and obey the Saviour's injunction to enter into our closets and shut our doors, for I am persuaded that much of the benefit of prayer is lost by trying to pray in the presence of others, or under any distracting circumstances, or in places where we are subject to interruption. Let there be some place, however small, where we can literally enter in and shut the door, beseeching God to enable us in shutting that to shut out the world also with it.

Let us recollect to whom we pray; his holiness, his power, his tenderness, his willingness to hear, his invitations to us to speak. Let us recall our own weakness and dependence, the wants of our bodies, the greater need of divine things for our souls; and then, with the implicit love and faith of little children, let us speak to him the very thoughts of our hearts.

For what shall we pray? Literally and definitely, for everything we want. Whatever we desire or need for ourselves, for our friends in the church or the world or the family, things material, things social, things spiritual, for the present or the future, for time or for eternity, let us ask for them in faith. As there is nothing so high or good that we may not ask for it, so there is nothing so lowly or small that God will despise it. Let us make known to him, our loving Father, *all* our wants. God has in no wise limited our petitions or his answers; it is we ourselves who limit them by wavering and want of belief.

> "Thou art coming to a King;
> Large petitions with thee bring,
> For his grace and power are such
> Thou canst never ask too much."

Spiritual Life: Prayer Answered.

"*Receive, I pray thee, the law from his mouth, and lay up his words in thine heart. For there shalt thou have thy delight in the Almighty, and shalt lift up thy face unto God; there shalt thou make thy prayer unto him, and he shall hear thee.*"—JOB xxii. 22, 26, 27.

CHAPTER VI.

Spiritual Life: Prayer Answered.

IT has already been asserted, regarding the things for which we shall pray, that we may ask, literally and confidently, for just what we want. God's covenant with those who pray in faith extends over the whole range of possibilities, as regards human wants and desires. It promises abundant food for the support of life. "Behold the fowls of the air, they sow not, neither do they reap, yet your heavenly Father feedeth them. Are ye not much better than they?" It promises appropriate raiment for the body. "Consider the lilies, how they grow. They toil not, they spin not, yet Solomon in all his glory was not arrayed like one of these. If, then, God so clothe

the grass, how much more will he clothe you." It promises the healing of diseases,* protection from pestilence,† strength to meet every demand,‡ wisdom for each event of life,§ escape from every temptation,|| comfort for every sorrow,¶ peace in the shadow of death,** and a glad welcome at the gates of heaven.†† All these are included in God's covenant with us, and if at any time the promise fails of fulfillment, we may be sure that it is because some of the conditions which belong to our share of the covenant are not performed.

The first requisite for success in prayer is *faith*. "Whatsoever ye ask in prayer, believing, ye shall receive." "But ask in faith, nothing wavering," and the answer will assuredly come. Sometimes, undoubtedly, it is long deferred, but we must remember that God in his great plans for us

* James v. 15. † Ps. xci. 5, 6. ‡ Deut. xxxiii. 25.
§ James i. 6. || 1 Cor. x. 13. ¶ 2 Cor. i. 4; Isa. lxvi. 13.
** Ps. xxiii. 4. †† Matt. xxv. 34.

and ours is not bounded by the feeble scope of a human mind. He sees beyond and above our farthest power of vision. He leads us in that way which will bring us most surely to a happy end and will produce in us the highest development of our moral nature. In material things we can often understand that God may withhold certain gifts from us lest they should prevent a spiritual blessing, which is just so much more important to us as the soul is greater than the body. Thus, we often pray for humility of mind, for forgetfulness of self, for more entire consecration to God, and in the same petition ask for certain earthly blessings which, if granted, might make us proud, selfish and worldly.

If God, then, loving his children and desiring their highest good, grants their better prayer, and by so doing is forced to deny their poorer one, shall we call him unfaithful? No; rather let us bless him for withholding evil from us and rest upon him with the heartfelt confidence that he not only hears, but also grants every faithful prayer that does not interfere with our true heavenward progress.

In spiritual things we are less able to understand God's long delays. Perhaps we are praying, year after year, for the conversion of a dear friend, and yet the answer is withheld till our hearts sink within us with anxiety and fear. But such prayers, we may implicitly believe, are never lost. God's time is not always our time; sometimes when we are ready "Jesus' hour is not yet come;" and while we are wondering at the long delay his plans are ripening hour by hour. Perhaps he is moulding the beloved soul we pray for into a more excellent frame for its true conversion to him at last, and is developing in us those graces of faith, perseverance and sole dependence on him which he delights to see in his children.

"The effectual, fervent prayer of a righteous man availeth much," but how much, eternity only can unfold, and it is not essential for us to know. God's command is, that we shall pray in earnest, child-like faith; his promise is, that he will hear and answer.

But let us watch with ceaseless vigilance against careless, heartless or formal praying. It is only a mockery to the most high God, and an idle repetition of words as concerns ourselves. Again and again we must say, as did the early disciples, "Lord, teach us to pray," and with the words of our souls, not the words of our lips, we must speak, for only that which comes out of our hearts can find its way into the great heart of the loving Father and turn it toward us.

Dr. Thomas Fuller, one of the wittiest and quaintest of old divines, has left a little meditation upon careless prayer, and the way in which such a habit increases upon us when once indulged, which is so widely applicable in the matter of its teaching and so clever in the style of its setting-forth that I quote it without alteration.

*"Pope Boniface the ninth, at the end of each hundred years, appointed a jubilee at Rome wherein people, bringing themselves and money thither, had pardon for their sins.

"But centenary years returned but seldom; popes were old before and covetous when they came to their place. Few had the happiness to fill their coffers with jubilee coin. Hereupon Clement the Sixth reduced it to every three and thirtieth, Paul the Second and Sixtus the Fourth to every twenty-fifth year.

"Yea, an agitation is reported in the conclave to bring down jubilees to fifteen, twelve or ten years, had not some cardinals (whose policy was above their covetousness) opposed it.

"I serve my prayers as they their jubilees. Perchance they may extend to a

* Fuller's "Good Thoughts in Bad Times."

quarter of an hour, when poured out at large. But some days I grudge this time as too much, and omit the preface of my prayer with some passages conceived less material, and run two or three petitions into one, so concentrating them to half a quarter of an hour.

"Not long after, this seems also too long. I decontract and abridge the abridgment of my prayers; yea (be it confessed to my shame and sorrow, that hereafter I may amend it), too often I shrink my prayers to a minute—to a moment—to a Lord have mercy upon me!"

There are many of us, I am afraid, who must plead guilty to an occasional haste and carelessness, almost if not quite as great as this; but surely there are none of us so irrational or presuming as to suppose that such praying deserves or receives an answer. The promise, as we have already said, is made to the faithful, fervent outpouring of the heart, and to all such petitions the response is sure and unfailing.

In fact, the actual answer to prayer is often so immediate and so minute that it is almost startling to the petitioner. Such instances are so frequent that it would take volumes upon volumes to contain them. In Muller's "Life of Faith" we have the history of a whole institution supported and carried on, day by day, through the earnest prayers of faithful men and God's immediate answers to them; and the experience of every Christian supplies more or less evidence of his wonderful replies to special petitions.

De Liefde's beautiful story of little Dirk, the widow's son, who prayed that God would send the ravens to them with bread, as he had once sent it to Elijah, and of the answer he received, is not more beautiful nor striking than thousands of similar events taking place about us every day. The narrative has often been repeated, and yet can never be recalled too often, of the poor old colored woman, sick and crippled, who could do little but suffer and pray. She selected one after another among her acquaintances, rich or poor, young or old, white or black, and prayed for them day by day, till God changed their hearts; finally twenty persons, the subjects of her fervent petitions for years, had been thus brought into the kingdom of God.

The evidences that come within our own experience, however, or that of our friends, seem more conclusive than the accounts of that which has happened to others—more satisfactory, nearer home, closer to our own hearts; and when we know a thing to be true, its teachings are far more forcible than when we only suppose it to be so.

A lady of great piety and almost saintly life lost a precious and only son during the war. He entered the army very young, and, although he was religious in principle, dutiful, faithful and lovely in character, he was not professedly a Christian. The latest letters received from him, before his death, however, breathed so truly the spirit of a child of God that she had full reason to believe that her Saviour was also the Saviour of her son. Under circumstances that made his death doubly distressing she was upheld most wonderfully; her mind was stayed on God, and he kept her in perfect peace.

After a while her health failed; her husband was away from home, and in her loneliness and sickness a terrible anxiety took possession of her with regard to the safety of her son's soul. For several days it beset her with agonizing force, till, at last, one dreary night it seemed almost to overwhelm her. She knelt and prayed with intense supplication that God would send peace to her heart in some way, in any way, and give her rest in thinking of her darling, so that she might lay aside this sickening terror. Then she lay down to sleep, but it seemed as if she had scarcely closed her eyes, when, upon suddenly opening them again, she saw her son standing by her bedside. He was dressed in his bright uniform, as when she saw him last, and was looking down at her with his old pleasant smile and a face beaming with love, and yet full of peace.

"Oh, Charley!" she exclaimed, "is this you?"

"Yes dear mother," he answered very gently; "I have been permitted to come to you for your comfort, to show you how well all things are with me."

"And won't you stay a little while?" she said; "I have so much to say to you."

"No, dear mother," he replied, even more tenderly than before; "I am under orders and may not delay. I have fulfilled my charge and I must go."

In an instant she awoke, so filled with joy and gratitude that she arose and kneeled again in thankful prayer.

"What if it was but a moment's dream?"

she said afterward; "God knows it was just what I needed, for my heart seemed breaking. From that day to this I have never had a doubt of my child's safety, nor should have had then, probably, had I not been sick and desolate, and unable to use my faith or reason. For that very cause my heavenly Father sent me a 'vision of peace' to soothe my sick heart; he gave me an immediate and satisfying answer to an agonized and almost despairing prayer."

But it is not solely in the answers to great and sorrow-laden prayers that God's faithfulness in responding fills the heart with surprise and gratitude. His goodness in hearing our less-important petitions is almost more striking; and in the incident that follows, though we may smile at the facts set forth, we cannot but thank our heavenly Father for taking such pains to teach a humble child:

A few years ago a friend had in her Sunday-school class a bright, affectionate boy whose early life had been entirely without religious influence. All such subjects were new to him; they seemed to open another world to his eyes, and his interest in them was very deep. He often came to see her on a week-day that they might be able to talk more freely and unreservedly than in the class. One afternoon they had been talking of prayer and God's sure answers to it, and she had been trying to inspire him with the same firm belief which she felt herself. But he was rather puzzled with it; it seemed to him too much to believe that the great God in heaven should trouble himself to hear and answer our little, insignificant prayers. Our great petitions, he thought, might claim more notice, but the little ones he "wouldn't bother about."

"But he has promised," she urged; "try it for yourself and see."

"I will," he answered with a bright look in his eyes; "I will try him and see."

"You would not, of course, mock God

with foolish prayers," she said; "that would not be right."

"But, teacher," he rejoined, "you say he likes to give us all the little things we want."

"I fully believe he does," she replied, "and that he gives them always unless it is against our truest good to do so."

"I'll try him," he said; but there was something about his look that puzzled and troubled her, and after he was gone she questioned with herself whether she had done wisely. But while earthly wisdom often fails God's wisdom never does.

A few days after came her boy again with a face as bright as the sun. He held something in his hands behind his back, and when she asked him what it was he replied, softly, "It is an answer to prayer." There never was a face that looked at the same time so perfectly radiant, so happy and yet so solemn. She almost trembled for a moment lest her teaching had been misunderstood or misapplied; then she said, "Tell me about it."

"Yes, it's an answer to prayer," he repeated, and taking his hands from behind him he laid in her lap a beautiful dead partridge, flecked and speckled with white and ashen tints on the soft brown with such heavenly art as only one hand has skill to use.

"You see, teacher, you looked so white and sick the other day when I was here, it seemed to me a nice broiled quail or partridge would taste nice to you and do you a lot of good, too; besides that, I wanted the fun of catching one. So I went home and prayed to God to send one into my snare. I could hardly expect it yet, you know, it's so early; the buckwheat's only just gone out of the field, and there's lots of wild berries and seeds left yet; but, thinks I, that don't make much difference if he has a mind to send it. So I prayed for it, and I prayed hard, too, for I thought if God should take the trouble to do this little thing I'd never mistrust him again. Well, in the morning when I went to the snare there had been one in and a fox or something had eaten it out. Its little soft feathers were scattered all about, and the snare and all were bitten right out. I felt pretty queer then, and I had to sit down on a stone under the cedar tree and think about it. It seemed like a big lesson. I was almost scared to think God had sent it there, and yet I felt awfully to have it gone. It made me think of what you said the other day of people who asked for things that did them no good and got them; you said the verse over twice about them, how God gave them the desire of their heart, and sent leanness into their soul. That was me, exactly. God had sent me that thing I wanted so much to show me he could do it, but now it was gone I felt worse than if it hadn't been there. So I kneeled down and told him I was sorry I had made such a foolish prayer, but I would stick to what I had said, anyhow, and never doubt him again; for though I was silly, I told him he'd taught me a big lesson; 'for,' said I, 'Lord, I do believe there was a partridge, or else a quail, in that snare; and, what's more, I do believe you could send another into it and keep the foxes from eating it up, too, if you had a mind to.' But I didn't ask him to. I wouldn't have asked him again for anything! And when I got there, this morning, there was this plump fellow, just dead, warm yet! This time I kneeled down and thanked him for sending such a fat bird for you, all out of his own goodness, when I didn't deserve it at all; and I'll never, never doubt him again!"

And, apparently, he never did. This had been a test of his own choosing, and the answer was a divine guarantee of faithfulness to his boyish mind.

And how can we, how dare we, mistrust God? We know he has the power to do what he will, and he tells us he has the will to use that power for us. Let us take him at his word, and rest in him. "I will set him on high, because he hath known my name. He shall call upon me, and I will answer him; I will be with him in trouble, I will deliver him and honor him. With long life will I satisfy him, and show him my salvation."

Spiritual Life: Bible Study.

"*Open thou mine eyes, that I may behold wondrous things out of thy law.*"—Ps. cxix. 18.

CHAPTER VII.

Spiritual Life: Bible Study.

THERE is a story in the Arabian Nights of a mysterious and powerful geni who by some magical means was imprisoned in a tiny vase; as soon as the cover was lifted he expanded with indescribable rapidity until he became an immense mass of cloud which no possible efforts could compress into the little vase again.

Every one who has ever been compelled by circumstances to condense a great subject into a small space knows just how difficult a task it must have been to imprison the geni in that little vase. We take a little word, a phrase, a text, for our subject, quite unconscious of all that lies within it; but suddenly, when we begin to break the seals and open its depths, it expands into a great theme which wise men have written volumes about and not exhausted. Such topics as we have been considering, and especially that which forms the subject of the present chapter, are such fruitful themes, and such important ones, that it is almost disheartening to try to limit them to such a tiny space only as can be allowed in a little volume like this. We must either necessarily leave out a great deal that might well be said or we must condense matters into a mere series of statistical utterances.

The Apostle Paul, it seems to me, was under just such a pressure of much to say and short time to say it in when he wrote the twelfth chapter of Romans. There, a whole Epistle, or rather, series of them, is condensed into a few verses: "He that giveth, let him do it with simplicity; he that ruleth, with diligence; he that showeth mercy, with cheerfulness; let love be without dissimulation. Abhor that which is evil; cleave to that which is good; not slothful in business; fervent in spirit; serving the Lord;" and so on through many verses.

But the Apostle Paul's power of condensation has not extended itself to every one, neither is it just the style best adapted for keeping the mind in thoughtful consideration of a single subject; we must therefore decide to select the principal points which occur to us in connection with it, while we leave many others to be thought out by the reader.

It is our duty and our pleasure to read the Bible, because it contains the revealed will of God; because we believe it to have been written by chosen men, under his direct guidance, to be the only revelation so made from God to man, and to contain all knowledge necessary to inform us of the plan of salvation, the requirements of God and the obligations of man.

The Scriptures should be read with faithful prayer, for only by the help of God's

Spirit can we hope rightly to understand his word. The heart of man is full of blindness and prejudice, and, left to itself, may distort the purest teachings. The Apostle Peter, even, speaks of the epistles of his beloved brother Paul as containing things which are hard to be understood and which the unlearned and the unstable wrest, as they do also the other Scriptures, to their own destruction.

In fact, when we consider the subject closely, we find there is hardly a schism, a heresy or a religious extravagance of any kind, of the many which have grown up during all the centuries of the Christian era, which has not had its rise in some Scripture precept or doctrine separated from its whole meaning and thereby losing its proper balance, and thus carried to an unreasonable extreme.

The Bible is a book of vast resources; its contents embrace almost every known form of writing; its histories, biographies, narratives, poems, prophecies, proverbs; its travels, its wars, its allegories, its precepts and its books of laws, aside from its more absolute spiritual teaching, render it a vast storehouse of information. Even the infidel cannot afford to lose the treasures of knowledge it contains, and accepts as truth the more material part, which he wants to make use of, while he scoffs at that which condemns his rebellious and unbelieving life.

Satan himself used perverted words of Scripture for argument in the temptation of our Saviour, and was foiled by the undistorted truths of the Bible from Christ's own lips. But, aside from the intentional perversion of Scripture, our own limited capacity and proneness to error render it necessary that we should have the aid of God's Spirit in order first to understand and then practice it rightly. This he gives us gladly and freely. "If ye, being evil, know how to give good gifts to your children, how much more shall your heavenly

Father give the Holy Spirit to them that ask him?"

There is a great deal of help which we may get from easy and open sources for intelligently reading the Bible, which yet is frequently quite overlooked. No one that has not tried it can ever imagine the difference between habitually reading a Bible with references and marginal readings and one that has neither. The Bible admirably explains itself; it makes the most striking commentary on itself; and to read it daily in this way gives a knowledge of its contents tenfold greater and more thorough than can be acquired by the simple, casual reading of a chapter. It certainly takes much more time, but it is surely better to read a few verses studiously and faithfully than a much larger portion without study. We learn to associate together verses and facts that belong together; to explain this by that and to balance one by another. So important does this manner of reading appear to us that it seems almost a waste of time and money to print and publish so many small Bibles without either references or marginal readings where a little more expended of both would give to the reader not only the word of God, but such admirable helps for comprehending it fully.

Valuable helps to Bible study are published so cheaply now by different religious societies that almost every one, even with limited means, is able to purchase the most essential of them. A good Bible atlas, Bible dictionary and concordance give a wonderful amount of help in properly understanding what we read; and, after these, come various well-known writers and commentators, whose works on different parts of the Scriptures have been of incalculable value to the world.

The faithful, daily reading of the Scriptures is essential for the spiritual progress of every Christian, but especially is it valuable in early life. If young people could only once understand how much less time for study they will have as they grow older, and how many more distractions, cares and hindrances; and how the weary mind, burdened with many thoughts, can but half take in the precious truths which the fresh young brain absorbs so eagerly, they would surely spare no effort to make themselves thoroughly conversant with the word of God in the days of their youth.

There is something wonderful in the effect which much Bible study has upon the character; it gives a strength, depth and clearness of judgment that no other study or pursuit ever can give. It imparts a steadfastness to weak minds and a balance to frivolous ones; it softens hard natures and purifies coarse ones, so that the intellectual part of man, as well as the spiritual, is vastly elevated and improved by it. And for our moral nature it is absolutely essential. We need its constant teachings to recall to us the words of our Saviour, to hold up before us repeatedly the loveliness of his life, to reimpress upon us the precepts, the injunctions, the instructions for our daily thinking, speaking and acting. We need it to be ever before our eyes as a standard of righteousness in an evil world, as a measure and a balance by which to weigh all things, as a criterion by which to test them.

In the "Paradise Lost" we are told that the angel Ithuriel found Satan in the form of a toad squatting close by Eve's ear that he might whisper evil into it as she slept, and that with one touch of his spear he restored him to his own proper shape again;

> For no falsehood can endure
> Touch of celestial temper, but returns
> Of force to its own likeness.

And in the Scriptures we have a surer agent for unveiling evil than even the heavenly spear of the angel; a more certain touchstone, which, applied to all that we can bring to it, strips off disguise, falsehood and pretence and displays the naked truth.

Let us bring to this ordeal, then, all that concerns us in this life—the requirements of our business, the customs of society, the amusements of the day; all questions of morals or of doctrines, new dogmas, strange teachings, the speeches of orators, the preaching of the pulpit, the assertions of books. Let us set them side by side with the revelation which God has given to man as the guide of his way, and, with that heavenly light shining upon them, conscientiously inquire into their true bearings and influence.

We must not, however, be misunderstood as implying that the Bible should be used as a test of the truth of works of science, art or history; it was given to teach us the plan of salvation, and not as a handbook of science. Its object is to present, for man's inspection and obedience, a standard of holy living, a code of laws of heavenly wisdom, and in all questions relating to right and wrong, to man's duty to God and his neighbor, to God's love and care toward man, to every shade of moral discussion, the Bible will be found an infallible guide, unerring, explicit and easily understood. "For if our gospel be hid, it is hid to them which are lost."

It would certainly be very remarkable to expect to find anything in the Scriptures discussed in a strictly scientific or technical way; its casual indefinite remarks upon all such topics should be looked upon as not intended to be either contradictory to or confirmatory of scientific truths, but simply as incidental to the grand object of its existence. Of one thing, however, we may be very sure—God's word will never and can never really contradict his works. They both spring from the same source, the eternal Fountain of might, knowledge and truth. We are often blind to the real meaning of God's words; we are yet deplorably ignorant of the least of his works; but when we come fully to understand both, we shall find a perfect harmony and fitness between them.

To repeat, then, concisely, what we have already dwelt upon, let our reading of the Scriptures be a daily act, let it be reverent, let it be prayerful, let it be studious, let it be wise, and let us learn to apply its teachings to every event of life, whether great or small. The more we study it the more we shall love it; the better we know it the plainer we shall see how little we still know; the deeper we search into its mines of treasure the vaster will its farther avenues and deeper depths appear to us. It is an inexhaustible source of study; and the oldest, wisest and most diligent of Bible students will tell you that he has but begun to know all its wonders. As John Jewell, bishop of Salisbury, wrote of the fullness of Holy Writ more than three hundred years ago, so those who know it best have found it ever since: "The word of God is the water of life—the more ye lave it forth the fresher it runneth; it is the fire of God's glory—the more ye blow it the clearer it burneth; it is the corn of the Lord's field—the better you grind it the more it yieldeth; it is the bread of heaven—the more it is broken and given forth the more it remaineth; it is the sword of the Spirit—the more it is scoured the brighter it shineth. The voice of God cannot be unpleasant to their ears who are the children of God—the oftener they hear it the more they receive; they can never have overmuch who never have enough."

Spiritual Life: Public Worship.

"*Not forsaking the assembling of ourselves together, as the manner of some is.*"—HEB. x. 25.

"*In all places where I record my name I will come unto thee, and I will bless thee.*"—EX. xx. 24.

CHAPTER VIII.

Spiritual Life: Public Worship.

IT is hardly a possible thing for the mind of man, at the present time, to make any approximate estimate of the benefit which has accrued to the world through the assembling together of Christians for the public worship of God. Could we picture ourselves in a state of society exempt from all influences of the public ordinances of the Church, either present or past, we should look upon a scene so strange as to be beyond recognition.

If devotion to God had been enjoined upon man as a private, secret exercise, to be entered upon exclusively within the closet or behind closed doors, our whole social existence would be changed. The grandest achievements of olden times in statuary and painting would be blotted out of being; they were not executed for the contemplation of solitary worshipers, but for the vast masses who met in great churches and praised God in choral anthems. The rarest music that we have, the hymns of the ages, whose strains have lost neither sweetness nor power by long and frequent use, would never have been composed. Our noblest works of architecture, cathedrals, minsters and churches, would have no existence. The hushed meetings of the early martyrs at dead of night with all their impending consequences for this world and the next, the bands of hunted Huguenots praying among the mountains, the covenanters singing their hymns among the rocks and heather of Scotland, half the pathos and pith of history, half its wars and its perils, half its deeds of prowess and its names of renown, would be lost to us for ever.

A silent, secret allegiance to God, acknowledged only in the heart of the family or quietly practiced in private life, would never have aroused the opposition, fury and bloodshed which have so often followed the open assembling of Christians and the public avowal of religious belief. If Nero and Diocletian, if Charles the Ninth and Philip the Second, if cruel Queen Mary of England and reckless King Charles, could have put an absolute stop to the gatherings of Christians their persecutions would probably have been suspended.

But God, who knows so well the heart of man, never showed his love and care for his children and his Church on earth more indisputably than when he enjoined and encouraged their public assembling together. As private devotion, meditation and study are essential to the growth of the individual Christian, so is public worship necessary to the growth of the Church. To look for a great increase of Christianity and spread of the gospel with each man worshiping God in his own house only, would be like expecting to conquer a country by sending isolated soldiers in upon it, and directing each to win his own rood of soil. There must be unity of purpose, there must be the consolidation of forces and there must be the sympathy, strength and enthusiasm which human beings communicate to each other when gathered into bands for a solemn purpose.

Without public worship the Sabbath would be an entirely different day from what it is at present; it might, indeed, remain a day of rest, but its chief occupation would be gone. No pleasant chimes would call willing hearts to the place of worship or ring reproachful tones into the ears of reckless men; no crowds of earnest Christians would tread the quiet streets, making an endless procession of witnesses to the world that God has many worshipers on earth and winning it to adore him with them by the force of silent example. The voice of the preacher, which now calls from week to week to the impenitent, would be silent, and one great means of the conversion of the world would be obliterated. The happy relationship between pastor and people, the gentle charities between rich and poor in the same congregation, the brotherhood of fellow-worshipers, arising from the affection and sympathy developed by the mere fact of praying side by side under one roof for years together, would be entirely done away with.

The great enterprises which have long been evangelizing the world, lighting up its dark places of cruelty, preaching the gospel to the ignorant at home and abroad, and in many ways lifting up the human race toward a purer and more spiritual life, could never have been organized by men single-handed. Christians help each other, inspire each other, encourage, cheer and urge each other on to good deeds and great efforts, and their influence is nowhere brought to bear so powerfully on each other as in social and public gatherings for worship.

But it is not Christians alone who should maintain the service of the Church; every creature on earth owes praise and homage to the Almighty, and should unite with the people of God in giving it. It is impossible, however, to ignore the fact, that multitudes who ought to go habitually to church, stay away, and that some of their reasons for so doing have a specious look of truth about them.

Church-going, they say, does not save souls; many a man goes through mere hypocrisy, and if God had meant us to keep the Sabbath in that way, he would have given more definite commands about it. Sometimes they even go so far as to say that such ceremonies belonged to the Mosaic law, and that law is done away with.

We may freely admit to them that church-going does not of necessity save souls, although we claim that a great many souls are saved by just that agency. And they will have to admit to us that if hypocrites and worldly people do go, they cannot hurt the church and may receive some benefit; while the fact of their going testifies to their conviction that there is at least an eminent respectability, solidity and excellence about ordinary church-goers, the aroma of which they would fain share with them. And as for the divine injunctions to keep the Sabbath holy and frequent the house of God for worship, they are as plain, repeated and incontrovertible as any other command whatever; and those who speak of Mosaic law must study their Bibles better and go far back of Moses, even to the first man Adam and his home in Paradise, to find the appointment of the Sabbath as a day of rest unto God.

The finger of the Almighty himself prepared the tables of stone and wrote upon them the ten commandments which Moses received on Mount Sinai; and the very wording of the fourth commandment, "Remember the Sabbath day to keep it holy," points back to a thing long ago established and known among men.

One of the most oft-repeated injunctions in the Old Testament is that concerning the keeping of the Sabbath holy, and in immediate connection with that is the frequenting of the sanctuary. "Keep my Sabbaths and reverence my sanctuaries; keep thy foot when thou goest to the house of God; praise God in the sanctuary; in the temple doth every one speak of his glory."

God rested on the seventh day and sanctified it; how soon men began to keep it holy by special offerings and worship we cannot tell. Probably very soon after the fall of man, for we find both Abel and Cain offering homage to God, one in accordance with and one against the appointed way, as if already such sacrifice and worship were an accustomed thing; and shortly after, in the days of Enos, Adam's grandson, we are told that men began to call themselves the children of God. Noah assembled his family for openly worshiping God when the flood was over, and Melchisedec, king of Salem, was also a "priest of the most high God." If a priest, we reason inferentially that there must have been devotions to lead, sacrifices to offer and an assembly to minister unto; and, as in numerous instances we find allusions to the seventh day as a day distinguished from others, we have reason to suppose that it was early set apart as a time for especial worship. Among the Israelites there were particular sacrifices and observances for that day, so that the Sabbath, as a period of rest, has been associated with the public worship of God and a "holy convocation" of the people from the earliest times.

God himself seems always to have made especial provision for the gathering together of congregations for united worship. As soon as the Israelites encamped in the wilderness, he ordered the fashioning and setting up of the tabernacle; when Canaan was possessed and the kingdom of Israel well established, he chose Mount Moriah in Jerusalem as the place where his house should be built, and instructed David in all that was necessary with regard to it. After the Jewish captivity and the destruction of Solomon's temple, he softened the heart of King Cyrus, who permitted the people under Ezra and Nehemiah to return and rebuild the temple. Among the Jews in later times, whenever in a small community there were even ten full-grown men, they were enjoined to build a place of worship.

Our Saviour upheld the keeping of the Sabbath, declaring that it was made for man; he bade the people search the Scriptures, which they could only do in those days of ignorance by frequenting the synagogues on the Sabbath day, where the Scriptures were read and expounded. He upheld public worship by going himself into the temple or the synagogues on the Sabbath and teaching the people. "*As his custom was*," St. Luke says, "he went into the synagogue on the Sabbath day and stood up for to read." St. Paul is several times spoken of as going into the synagogues on the Sabbath day to preach to the people; so that we have commands, injunctions, examples, besides all that we gather inferentially, going to prove that public worship is pleasing to God and forms a large part of the keeping of the Sabbath according to his will.

We have already referred in the early part of this chapter to the excellent effect of habitual public worship upon the individual Christian in developing many phases of character that might otherwise lie dormant, and to its silent but powerful influence upon the world, and there are one or two thoughts in connection with this that seem worthy of a place in its close. Older Christians know, but younger ones find it hard to believe, that it makes comparatively little difference in our spiritual growth whether the preaching under which we sit is eloquent or homely; whether the preacher to whom we listen is very congenial to our tastes and character or the reverse. Probably among persons of more than average refinement and culture, in many cases, the preaching which falls to their lot is not especially to their liking. How can it be otherwise? While they may respect and honor every good man, and especially every faithful minister of the gospel, there may be an entire want of congeniality in some respects between them. They may approve heartily of all he says, and yet his manner of saying it may jar a little upon some sensitive point. So they seek for some preacher a little more eloquent or a little more congenial in some neighboring church, and the result is that there has come to be in these days a great amount of wandering away from old influences, a severing of old ties, in the search for something more original or more interesting than could be found at home.

Such a habit as this is very unprofitable spiritually, however popular. We have fallen into a way of looking entirely too much to the preacher as the central point in public worship and too little to the people. The main object of assembling ourselves in congregations is not to hear the eloquence of man or be pleased and startled with his originality. If Providence has so happily ordered our lot that in the way of simple duty and custom we may listen to the words of one of the mighty men of the Church, we have reason to be greatly thankful. If not, let us remember that the chief obligations and benefits of public worship remain unchanged.

We meet together to express openly our homage to God, to unite with fellow Christians in hymns of praise to his name, to coöperate with them in plans of active benevolence, to join them in thanksgiving for his mercies, in pleadings for pardon, in supplication for his continued love and care, and to think upon some fact connected with eternal things presented to us by him who ministers to us. However the subject may be put before us, whether richly or poorly, God's word remains the same, and we must take it into our hearts and ponder it.

Thoroughly to enjoy and profit by public worship it is not needful that the preaching be brilliant, the prayers eloquent or the music scientific. Little is wanted in those external things, but much *in ourselves.* A willing mind, a peaceful frame, a childlike heart, full of love toward God and man, will render all God's service a blessing and a delight, and every Sabbath as peaceful as the eternal one above.

Wherever, then, it has pleased God to appoint our lot let us remain until his voice calls us to a different sphere. Let us devoutly join in the public worship of God's house, in the companionship of kindred and friends; let us sustain the influence of our pastor by every means in our power, responding to every call, ready for every good work, and willingly ministering unto him in both spiritual and temporal things as we have opportunity. Every church-member weakens or strengthens the church to which he belongs by withholding or giving his influence. A church divided against itself cannot stand, its worship will be cold, its works few; but let all the great evangelizing enterprises testify to what can be done by a united church, where pastor and people stand together, and work as one man for a good cause. It gathers mission-schools, it sends out Bible-readers, it establishes prayer-meetings, it founds charities, it plants churches, it provides work for all its members, and the public worship of God is best carried out and followed up with earnest works of practical Christianity.

Spiritual Life: Fruits of the Spirit.

"*Now the works of the flesh are manifest, ... of the which I tell you before, as I have also told you in time past, that they which do such things shall not inherit the kingdom of God. But the fruit of the Spirit is love, joy, peace, long-suffering, gentleness, goodness, faith, meekness, temperance.*"
—GAL. v. 19–23.

CHAPTER IX.

Fruits of the Spirit.

A GREAT deal of time has been wasted, a vast amount of imagination expended and innumerable far-fetched theories put forth in speculations as to the different conditions of heaven and hell, and the elements which combine to make the one a place of joy, the other a place of horror. It has often seemed to me that St. Paul has suggested to us a vivid picture of each in his Epistle to the Galatians, where he says: "Now the works of the flesh are manifest, which are these, Adultery, fornication, uncleanness, lasciviousness, idolatry, witchcraft, hatred, variance, emulations, wrath, strife, seditions, heresies, envyings, murders, drunkenness, revellings and such like: of the which I tell you before, as I have also told you in time past, that they which do such things shall not inherit the kingdom of God. But the fruit of the Spirit is love, joy, peace, long-suffering, gentleness, goodness, faith, meekness, temperance." Gal. v. 19–23.

Imagine a place where the works of the flesh—that is, the works of the unregenerate heart, for our poor flesh and blood would be innocent enough were it not for the sin-tainted soul that rules within,—imagine a place where such works were allowed full sway, indulged without check or hindrance, unmitigated by occasional gleams of good or by the hopes of ultimate relief. Imagine another where every heart glows with the pure warmth and clear light of a sanctified nature; where every noble aspiration, every intellectual taste, every unselfish purpose, every true affection is developed and exalted—where not one fear shakes the security and not one sin mars the perfection. Add to these, in one place, the vast displeasure of the eternal God resting with terrible might upon each rebellious soul; in the other, his fatherly love and blessed presence shining upon his children; and what can imagination produce that equals these two scenes in the height and depth of their happiness and their woe?

It is sometimes very remarkable to hear persons express the hope of finally reaching heaven, whose lives on earth prove that they could not be happy were they to go there; they possess none of the heavenly characteristics which would make it a congenial abode for them. If our blessed Lord were to take bodily to the rest of the saints a rebellious, blasphemous, evil-hearted man, he would be of all souls most miserable. Violence, impurity and greed were his ruling passions on earth, and God's pure heaven has nothing to gratify them.

As the tree falls, there it must lie. The mere fact of death overtaking the body has no moral effect upon the soul; it lives on its own life beyond the grave as it lived it here; he that is unjust and he that is filthy remain unjust and filthy still; he that is righteous and he that is holy, let them be righteous and holy still—the same, but intensified: the righteous soul, freed from temptation, secure for ever, alive in Christ; the rebellious soul, shut out from all hope at last, more desperate, more dead in sin.

To be happy in heaven, that great, wonderful home of God's children, toward which our eyes look, our hopes aspire and our hearts ascend—to be fitted for it, we must needs be heavenly-minded here; we must nourish those graces, those attributes, those affections, which will flourish in the pure atmosphere of heaven. By nature we cannot have them, by God's grace we may; the natural stock is poor and unworthy, but God has made it capable of receiving the engrafted word which is able to save our souls.

The nurseryman, with faith and patience

that can look through long years of toil and not be discouraged, plants the seeds of certain fruit trees. When his seedlings have grown to a foot or more in height he sees that of themselves they will never make fine trees nor produce good fruit. In fact, he knew it before, and only expected to secure good stock for grafting superior fruit upon. When the time arrives, therefore, he cuts off the whole top of his little trees and engrafts choice varieties upon them. Then he digs about them, enriches the soil, supplies them with moisture, frees them from insects, prunes them year after year, trains, trims and watches with indefatigable care till the trees reward him by bringing forth abundantly the beautiful fruit for which he has so long been waiting.

It is thus, in a measure, that the divine Husbandman deals with the plants in his vineyard. We have been considering in successive chapters the conversion of the soul or its reception of the "engrafted word," its manner of growth, the standard to which it should attain, the different phases of its outer and its inner life and the divers means of development and perfection which God has given.

We come now, therefore, to the results which the husbandman may well expect to find as the effect of his patient training, the fruits of the plants he has so watched and nourished. What shall the Lord of the vineyard say if he find them not at his coming?

They are called the fruits of the Spirit, the results of the operation of the Holy Ghost in our hearts, and they are essentially spiritual graces as shown in the life.

It is easier to every one of us human beings to exert ourselves for the accomplishment of a great feat than to labor on in silence with petty obstacles and little contests. It is grander, more fame-giving, to take a city than to rule one's spirit, but to rule one's spirit, God's word says, is the better of the two. It is easier to comply with all demands for the external fulfillment of religious exercises than patiently to war and struggle with the secret sins of our hearts. We cannot all win renown as did David in his youth by slaying a lion and a bear, but it is a duty that falls to each one of us to take the little foxes, the sly little foxes that spoil the vines and eat the tender grapes.

"To obey is better than sacrifice and to hearken than the fat of rams;" for it is the mind only which renders the outer works of any avail. Let us see, then, what that mind is which the Spirit can give, what those frames and affections are which the Master requires of us.

As the first fruit of the Spirit we are bidden to have love—thank God for inspiring the Apostle Paul to put that first on the list!—love toward God and man; that love which forgets itself, which freely gives itself, and which above all other things is more blessed in giving than in receiving; that faithful, fervent, pure affection which is called greater than faith or hope.

We are bidden to have joy, and I wish that every dreary, despondent Christian in the world would dwell on that thought until it dwells in him. Who can be, who should be, so joyful as God's children?—for they have such a sure rest, such a firm foundation of happiness, such promise of the life that now is and that which is to come.

We are bidden to have peace. What! in this turbulent, sorrowful, changing world? Yes, all restless, storm-tossed souls may find quietness in simply leaning upon the words of Christ. He has promised to give his peace unto us, not as the world giveth, not grudgingly, not scantily, not to be returned again, but abundantly of that peace of God which passes all understanding.

Long-suffering for every trying thing that meets us; for the fretting, chafing tempers of those about us, for the coldness or ingratitude of friends, for the malice of foes, for the tedious pains of sickness, for the wearying cares of life.

Gentleness—oh beautiful, wonderful word! —almost more a flower than a fruit of Christian life, in its grace and beauty adorning the rough places of the road, leading little children, lifting sad hearts, wiping away tears and winning wayward souls. St. Paul, with all his great and eloquent words, never melts the heart so truly as when he says, with an irresistible appeal, "I, Paul, beseech you by the gentleness of Christ."

Goodness, the staunch upholding of the right against the wrong at all hazards, the steadfast clinging to principle in the face of sharp temptation, the deliberate choosing of that which is hard and belongs to the soldier of the cross rather than that which is easy and of the world—a very bread-fruit among the other fruits of the Spirit.

Faith, the unshaken trust of the child in its Father, the confident assurance that He whose hand he holds and who holds his in return will lead him straight on through all that may await him, and bring him safely home at last; the unfaltering heart that leaves all to God; the unswerving eye that looks only unto him; the willing feet that follow unquestioningly where he calls and walk with the assurance of a victor in the strife through all. Faith is the golden apple among the fruits.

Meekness, a grace to be well thought of by disputatious Christians who love their racy theological arguments, and find a spicy pleasure in opposing themselves to others; a word for the every-day business of life abroad; a word for the household intercourse at home; a word for those in authority, that they may "in meekness instruct those that oppose themselves;" a word for those who are subordinate, that they may "receive the word with meekness;" a word for all, that they may show "all meekness to all men."

Temperance, the moderation of the wise

heart in all things; of the sanctified heart that knows how many things are lawful which yet are not expedient; of the strong, well-stayed heart, capable of self-denial and self-restraint, that refuses for itself a surfeit of any earthly thing whatever, knowing that the wants of the body are best supplied with temperate wisdom, and that the wants of the soul can be fully satisfied in God alone.

Wonderful and varied fruits of the Spirit! Well may the apostle say of those who possess them, "Against such there is no law." They enable us to do good to men, to glorify God, and to have peace in our own hearts; they make us meet for heaven; they please the Saviour who redeemed us, for he loves the souls of his children. St. John declared that he had "no greater joy than to hear that his children walked in truth." How much deeper and tenderer then the interest of our Lord in the progress of the children of his kingdom! How much stronger his desire to behold these fruits of the Spirit in their redeemed souls! How can we best gain them, keep them, develop them and show them forth as he would have us?

The way is simple, the way is old, long-discovered, prized by few, neglected by the many, but never changing, never closed. The old, old way to heaven is the way to sanctification; the way to glory is also the way to these heavenly graces, and all is found in Christ our Lord.

Looking to him, resting in him, abiding with him is the part of the soul; his tender grace and mercy do all the rest. "I am the true vine and my Father is the husbandman. I am the true vine, ye are the branches. He that abideth in me and I in him, the same bringeth forth much fruit; for without me ye can do nothing. Herein is my Father glorified, that ye bear much fruit."

Practical Life: The Christian at Home.

"*Let them learn first to show piety at home and requite their parents; for that is good and acceptable before God.*"—
1 TIM. v. 4.

CHAPTER X.

The Christian at Home.

THERE is no place on earth so like to heaven in its rest, its peace and its happiness as a lovely Christian family, where every member exhibits unselfish affection, sympathy and helpfulness. But, alas! how easy it is to disturb its quiet and mar its beauty! One person who indulges an irritable temper or an unruly tongue can take away all its serenity. Piety, like charity, should begin at home; like charity, too, it should not end there; yet we often find that persons who are most zealous abroad for the advancement of Christ's kingdom and the progress of every good work are most careless at home in maintaining a lovely and Christ-like demeanor.

It has often seemed to me that there are not many greater obstacles to the rapid growth of Christ's kingdom than the irritable and repelling conduct of some Christians in their private life. The household is the nursery of the Lord; children and servants there receive their first and deepest impressions of the power of the gospel over the daily life, and are attracted or repulsed according to the manifestations of Christian character which they see in the intimate relations of the family. It is amazing to find that good and thoughtful people can so overlook their responsibility toward those immediately about them; and yet it is a fact that many sincere Christians, whose piety is above suspicion, whose principles are steadfast and whose works of benevolence much to be commended, have not enough of the more gentle graces of the Spirit to keep them pleasant at home.

Abroad, the fact of being among comparative strangers induces reserve and self-restraint, and prompts the desire to please and conciliate. Besides this, the constant chafing of family cares, anxieties and fatigues is withdrawn and the mind is more at rest. But at home the yoke galls and they fret under it; duties are wearisome, and they fulfill them impatiently; something goes wrong, and they give way to petulance and fault-finding; they omit small self-restraints; they fail to check that "little member," the tongue, which St. James says is a fire, an unruly evil, full of deadly poison; and that little member unmastered soon becomes master himself, so that it often happens that the very one of the household whose example might most surely win and soften and bless all the rest comes at last to be like the dreaded Hymeneus, whose words eat as doth a canker.

The higher up in the household the unhappy influence is the more powerful is its effect on the whole family; but it is not possible for any member of any family to be so small or so insignificant as not to possess a vast power for good or for evil in the fireside circle to which he belongs. "Even a child is known by his doings, whether his work be pure and whether it be right." Gideon tried once to excuse himself from the mission of vengeance upon the Midianites, to which God called him, by pleading that his family was poor in the tribe of Manasseh and he "the least of his father's house;" but he was sent, while greater ones were passed by, and he was found well worthy of the name the angel gave him of "mighty man of valor." Jeremiah was afraid when God told him that he had ordained him a prophet unto the nations, and he cried, "O Lord God, behold I cannot speak; for I am a child!" But God sent him and helped him, and he spoke his words with great power.

We are almost forced to believe that there is nothing really small in all of God's plans, in all the events of our lives, in all the endless workings of the mind of man. We call some sins little sins, we estimate some victories over ourselves as little victories, but who, save God, can tell the unending influence they have upon our souls?

There is no human being insignificant in God's sight; we may think ourselves small, or mean, or useless, but let us remember that God respects no persons, but watches all hearts. The training and development of the immortal soul, and its ultimate perfection and salvation, are always of vast import in his sight; no less so in the tiniest child or poorest slave than in the conquerors and heroes of the world. That alone which gives any worth to the highest, gives equal worth to the lowest—the *deathless spirit* within. Let us not dare, then, to call ourselves powerless while we possess that which our Saviour said outweighed the gain of the whole world, but rather remember that our responsibility is great, our sphere great, our mission great, our influence great. Though we may be least in our Father's house, like Gideon;

though we be children in feeling, like Jeremiah; though we be weak in bodily presence, like Paul,—we have each a work to do, "a charge to keep," given us by God, and in his strength we shall be able to do it.

The household circle is especially the place where young Christians may exhibit a consistent bearing and conversation. Later years bring more demands upon them from the world and open to them other spheres of duty and usefulness; until that time comes, "Let them show piety at home," as our motto says, and "requite their parents."

The virtues and graces which require to be practiced in our quiet daily life are of a very simple, straightforward and, sometimes, almost of a homely kind. The family is a little community by itself, and one member has no right to do that which trespasses upon the time or the convenience of the others.

"'Cleanliness is next to godliness,'" said a friend lately, "is a proverb that was so faithfully rung in my ears when they were growing, that they have never lost the last echo of it. As it came from the lips of a very pious woman, I naturally concluded it was a scriptural assertion, and made a long search for it one day, with Bible and concordance, and finding no trace of it, told her of my disappointment. 'Write it on the cover then, child,' was the undaunted reply, 'for surely cleanliness is next to godliness.'"

If people only knew the trouble, the vexation to servants, the extra work, the confusion in the whole family, caused by such little commonplace faults as a want of cleanliness, order and promptness, surely they would cultivate those convenient virtues with hearty readiness. A few days since, a lucky or unlucky draught blew open the door of a room in which a dear young man of lovely temper and blameless life had been dressing for a little pleasure excursion. A coat, a vest, pantaloons, undergarments and a pair of boots lay in five separate lumps on the floor; two chairs were occupied with clothing he had taken out and concluded not to wear; a soiled collar and discarded cravat adorned the toilet-table; the four small drawers and three large ones of the bureau all stood agape at different stages of protrusion; the closet door was flung wide open; the water facet was running, and the whole appearance of the room seemed to indicate that a general chaos was impending.

"Order was heaven's first law," we are told, but it is the last in the code of many Christians, and omitted altogether in that of others. Confusion never rights itself; tired hands and weary feet must patiently restore order by extra effort, and faults tiny in themselves become giants when they oppress or distress other people.

Even our religious duties should be so arranged as not to interfere with the comfort of those about us. An eccentric old gentleman among our friends has a habit of taking very irregular hours for the practice of his private devotions. He enters into his closet and shuts the door; but that being done, in order effectually to drown any small noises that might creep through the key-hole, he proceeds to read and pray in such stentorian tones that conversation in the adjoining rooms has to cease: babies can't go to sleep, and visitors have to be sent away from the door, till the somewhat obtrusive exercise is over. He claims that far greater benefit is thus derived to his soul than by less audible exercises, but even were this so, can he be sure it outweighs the discomfort given to others? That is the truest love to God which blends with love to man; that is the sincerest goodness which forgets itself and ministers to the wants of others; and selfishness in religious things is no less blamable than in worldly matters.

A young lady, who had been brought up in a church whose forms were few and whose service was simple, became a very zealous Episcopalian. When Lent drew near and she found that early prayers were to be held in a church more than a mile away from home, nothing could deter her from going. Her father had an especial liking for having his children all about him at breakfast and family prayers, but that could not stop her. Her health had been delicate, and her physician forbade her taking such a long walk and sitting in a cold church before breakfast. Still she went. The family was large; the father had to go to his business, the children to school, the mother to her manifold occupations, the servants to their work; yet, morning after morning, for weeks, this zealous young woman had to have a late breakfast, served hot, to warm her after her exposure and fatigue; several times she fainted away in the hall from over-exertion before she could get to her room, and when Lent was over her father had the expense and trouble of sending her away on a little jaunt to recruit her wasted strength.

The services of every evangelical church are to be respected and approved, and undoubtedly early prayers are of great benefit to those whose time, health and family arrangements permit to attend them, but no one can deny that this mistaken girl was both doing and receiving harm. She thwarted her father, annoyed her mother, imposed extra work on the servants, trifled with her own health and set a miserable example to her younger brothers and sisters, in the most obstinate and selfish way, and all under the plea of fulfilling a religious duty. "Let them learn first to show piety at home and to requite their parents."

The household is not the place for ostentatious deeds; its life is made up of little things; its opportunities for self-denial and usefulness are constant but inconspicuous; its work as incessant and silent as the shining of the sun. In our home life, toward superiors there should be manifested reverence and obedience; toward equals, sympathy and ready help; toward inferiors, the gentle consideration which every noble heart delights to show to those in a position of dependence. Toward all, patience, love, cheerfulness and forgetfulness of self. Faith, hope and charity are three of the grandest attributes that belong to the Church on earth; but gentleness, patience and self-sacrifice are three household angels that whisper and sing and smile their way into all hearts, and win them to love what is right. All the sermons that have ever been preached have not brought as many souls into the kingdom of God as the sweet and patient daily life of his faithful children. We sometimes complain that our words are almost unheeded by those whom we are trying to influence; but, leaving that to Him who has promised to bless every earnest effort, let us concentrate more thought upon showing in our own lives how lovely, pure and true the religion of Jesus can make his followers, for in that way we shall print an indelible lesson upon their hearts, whether they will or no.

A little girl said to her teacher not long ago, "Our Lizzie has got to be a Christian."

"How glad I am!" was the reply.

"But I'm not," she rejoined; "I'm sorry. She isn't half as nice as she was before. I suppose she's pious and good, but she's so ugly-good! She reads big, solemn books, and hushes me up when I talk, and won't do a thing to amuse me; she tells me of my faults all the time, and isn't half as pleasant as she used to be. She isn't bad, you know, only just ugly-good!"

Ugly-good! Have we not had reason to apply the child's quaint epithet many times, both to ourselves and to others? That severe sort of virtue which cuts its straight path directly through the wishes, comfort and feelings of other people may be like the march of a conqueror, but, like that too, it leaves desolation behind it.

"The wisdom that is from above is first pure, then peaceable, gentle, easy to be entreated, full of mercy and good fruits, without wrangling (marginal) and without hypocrisy." The commands of Jesus go far beyond a loving behavior to those who love us. His words are, "Love your enemies, do good to them which hate you, bless them that curse you and pray for them which despitefully use you; and your reward shall be great, and ye shall be the children of the highest; for he is kind unto the unthankful and the evil."

The influences of home go with us all, both old and young, to the day of our death, and on, beyond, for ever. As our eyes take in unconsciously the sight of familiar objects, and our ears the hearing of well-known sounds, so our hearts are receiving, day by day and hour by hour, the incessant, though unnoticed, influences of home for good or for evil. There is no escape from them for large or small; the tiniest child feels them, though not knowing how or what it feels, and is drinking in constant draughts of that which shall purify him and make him good and happy, or which shall sadden and harden him.

A young boy of very amiable character was taken away from an unhappy home and a wicked mother, whose cruelty and violence had embittered all his early childhood, and was placed in a religious family. The mistress of the house, whose sympathy had been much touched by his previous wretchedness, took great pains to show affection and kindness to him, and to teach him frequently about good things. His loving heart and quick mind, so long cramped and chilled, seemed to expand and develop, like long-waiting blossoms in the warmth of spring.

They were in the habit of often reading the Bible together in the evening, and one night, after the lady's return from a short journey, when the chapter was finished, the child looked up in her face and said gratefully, "What a happy home this is, and how dreadful that one was! I have been thinking it must be only the difference between you and her. While you were away the whole house was sad; when she used to go away everybody was only afraid she would come back too soon. I sometimes think she was like the pillar of cloud before the Israelites, that was dark even in the sunlight; and you are like the beautiful pillar of fire, that made everything bright even at night."

Shall we be pillars of cloud or of fire in our homes? Shall we darken its brightness or brighten its darkness? There can be but one answer, one desire on that point, in every Christian heart. To accomplish it let us give up our wills, relinquish our own plans, bridle our tongues, subdue our tempers; let us show unfailing sympathy, affection, patience and cheerfulness; let us bear one another's burdens, and forgive one another's faults, and then we shall know and feel "how good and pleasant it is for brethren to dwell together in unity."

Practical Life: The Christian in the World.

"*He that walketh righteously and speaketh uprightly, he that despiseth the gain of deceits, that shaketh his hands from holding of bribes, that stoppeth his ears from hearing of blood and shutteth his eyes from seeing evil, he shall dwell on high; bread shall be given him; his water shall be sure. Thine eyes shall see the King in his beauty; they shall behold the land that is very far off.*"—ISA. xxxiii. 15, 16, 17.

CHAPTER XI.

The Christian in the World.

A LADY was one day passing a garden-plot belonging to the mother of one of her Sunday-school scholars, and, chancing to look over the fence, she saw that it looked very like the field of the slothful, for, lo! it was all grown over with thorns, and nettles had covered the face thereof.

Knee-deep in the wild, rank growth stood the scholar himself, thrashing away at it with a great stick.

"What are you doing, Jack?" said his teacher. "Are you playing or working?"

"Fighting weeds!" he exclaimed, breathlessly, lashing away with redoubled vigor—"fighting weeds!"

"It's rather late for that," she answered;

"they are half as tall as you are; you ought to have begun six weeks ago."

"That's true," he said, "but I didn't, and now all I can do is to take their old heads off before the seeds get ripe. They've choked out one crop already, and they've got to go!"

"You must begin earlier the next time," she replied; "and, meanwhile, Jack, don't be discouraged, for half the world is at the same work."

"What work, ma'am?" asked Jack.

"Why, fighting weeds, of course. Everybody is fighting them, except those who are letting them grow."

"Ah," said Jack, "I guess you don't mean black-weed and clover, that choke out cabbages. I guess you mean some of those things we had in our lesson last Sunday that choke out the good seed. I never thought of it in that way before!" And he looked around rather ruefully at the wild growth about him, while the lady passed on, leaving him to think of the double combat that awaited him.

Many Christians seem quite to overlook the fact that our whole course through this world must be, in a measure, a long conflict. Not a hopeless one, for we have the assurance of victory at the end; not a sad one, for we fight in a good cause; not a solitary one, for beloved comrades march with us, help us and receive our aid in return. Still, it is a conflict. Our mortal nature keeps its little germs of evil, its tiny seeds of sinful inclinations; and as soon as we sit down at ease they sprout and spread. The earlier we crush them, the easier and the more economical the process. "The beginning of strife," says Solomon, "is as when one letteth out water," and the same is more momentously true of all evil.

In those great levees that line the lower Mississippi, if a mole does but burrow through, so that the tiniest stream of water can find a direct passage, however small, it works and washes a way for itself with such wonderful rapidity that, if not quickly discovered and checked, an enormous crevice, a deluge of water and the flooding of miles and miles of low land are certain to ensue. So it is with all sin; it is a greedy and an aggressive foe; if we allow it but a little vantage ground, it takes more and more, till it possesses all.

It is like the camel who piteously entreated leave just to put his head under the flap of the tent where his master was sleeping with his little children, to shelter it from the storm, and when that permission was kindly given he went on to thrust in his neck and shoulders and fore-legs and ugly hump, and, finally, his whole body, taking possession of tent, robes, skins and all, and pushing out master and children into the tempest.

Or it is like an enormous wedge, slender, smooth and subtile at one end, monstrous and unwieldy at the other; but grant the thin, fine edge one little opening and the rest is sure to follow.

We cannot, then, too carefully watch the beginnings of evil, the first stirring of the small temptations that assail us; the result, both to the Church and the world, would be inestimably blessed if young Christians would only early form the habit of watching for and resisting them. Little deviations from the absolute truth; little swervings from the straightforward way of dealing; little yieldings to the worldly advice or example of others, are all, apparently, very little in themselves, are all, truly, only the narrow edge of the wedge.

At home the Christian is prone to a class of minor faults, such as fretfulness, impatience and selfishness. Abroad the temptations are deeper and far more momentous. In almost every respectable household there are strong sheltering protections that shut out the coarser and more decided temptations to sin with which we meet in the world, and an atmosphere of far greater refinement than men find in the resorts of business or amusement. But in the world there is no such artificial protection. A man's shield must be the shield of faith, and his breastplate that of righteousness, if he would be proof against the assaults that shall be made upon him.

There is not a calling of any kind, however honorable in name, that does not admit of unfair dealing and ungodly action, if the man who follows it has the inclination to practice them. There is none so humble or low that it cannot be made honorable and estimable by the integrity and perfect uprightness of those who engage in it. There is no business, either high or low, that can demand anything wrong for its legitimate pursuit; or, if that comes within range of its necessities, it is no business for a Christian to follow. Our standard of right should be simply the standard of the Bible. Custom, or the example of others, can never make that right which is essentially wrong, and yet custom and the example of others are two of the most insidious, irresistible and bewildering foes that ever meet us in the world.

It is the same with public amusements as with business. Because certain places of recreation are frequented by hundreds of people whom we like or respect, it seems reason enough, on the outside, why we should go too; here again we must bring the matter under consideration to the test of the Scriptures alone. As perfect honor, truth and integrity are the first attributes demanded of the Christian in his business, so perfect purity, sobriety and great moderation should be the chief characteristics of his amusements.

The standard of right and wrong has already been established by a divine Lawgiver; his decrees are pronounced with unmistakable precision in his own moral code; and no approbation of the world, no example of the majority, no authority of custom, can make good that which he calls evil. "Ye shall do no unrighteousness in judgment, in mete-yard, in weight or in measure. Ye shall not steal, neither deal falsely, neither lie one to another." And he "that walketh uprightly and worketh righteousness, that backbiteth not with his tongue, that doeth no evil to his neighbor, that honoreth them that fear the Lord, that sweareth to his own hurt and changeth not, that putteth not out his money to usury nor taketh reward against the innocent, he that doeth these things shall never be moved."

The word of God does not condemn, but rather commends, the industrious exercise of some daily pursuit. It bids us provide what is honest in the sight of all men, to owe no man anything, to be not slothful in business. It tells us that the hand of the diligent maketh rich and the diligent in business shall stand before kings. In the very Decalogue itself the injunction to rest on the

Sabbath day is no more explicit than the other half of the command, "Six days shalt thou labor."

We have reason to believe that God is pleased to have us exercise the numerous wonderful attributes of mind and body which he himself has bestowed upon us; the prudence, caution, intelligence and judgment, the powers of invention, of construction and of imitation; the skill of hand or quickness of eye or correctness of ear. They are all his gifts, not to be laid in a napkin and buried away out of sight, but to be used to the very best of our ability.

It is a very trite old saying that "what is worth doing at all is worth doing well;" many people have written it in their copy-books at school; more people still have heard it said dozens of times; everybody assents to it as a matter of course, yet not one person in twenty puts it in practice. It should be written in letters of gold in every house, in every school, in every shop, office and factory. To slight our work is to despise the task God has given us to do and to refuse the use of those powers he has given us to work with. If we have nothing but rag-picking or paper-sorting to do, it should be done as carefully and conscientiously as if it were the most important work in the world. He that is faithful in that which is least is faithful also in that which is greatest; he naturally grows to be so from his fidelity in small things.

Neglect of our present work unfits us for future work. There was once a certain clergyman who had charge of a small parish of very poor and plain people. Unlike most of the members of his profession, whose devotion and unselfish labor are unmistakable, he was rather anxious for a prominent position in the ministry, and his grand aim seemed to be to prepare himself for such a place. His people were simple and ignorant; he was studious and ambitious; he wrote the most scholarly discourses he was capable of, and delivered them with oratorical precision. The people yawned in his face Sunday after Sunday, and finally stayed away. The emptier the benches grew the more vehement became the preacher's gesticulations, and the louder his denunciations of those modern transgressors who, like the "diluvian sinners," would not listen to the "preacher of righteousness;" or else they seemed louder on account of the reverberation through the vacant space. He was kindly remonstrated with by an elder of his church, and reminded of the simplicity and ignorance of his people. "In fact, my dear sir," said the elder, courteously, "you are aiming too high to hit such a lowly mark; your sermons are beyond their understanding, they fly over their heads."

"I have thought of all that," returned the minister, "and I cannot believe it is my duty to lower my standard of preaching for a set of poor, uneducated people whom I shall not be with long. I must be thinking of my future career, of future usefulness, and cannot afford to waste all this time in writing simple sermons that will be of no further use to me, besides injuring the style I am acquiring for more cultivated hearers."

The elder represented to him that it could scarcely injure any man's style of writing to be obliged to put his thoughts into the simplest English, but rather an improving exercise; and that whether the style was improved or no, the souls of the people were suffering for want of nourishment; the fruit was hung too high, and they could not reach it.

"Let them lift themselves up to it, then," said the other. "We cannot raise them by lowering ourselves; let them lift themselves up to it."

Poor people and poor preacher! The congregation starved until famine made them bold, and then they parted with their pastor. He found another charge of simple people too, and pursued the same course with them; and, at the last accounts, he was still wandering about at cross-purposes with the world, full of a bitter sense of injury at his want of success, and, probably, still looking for that cultivated congregation whose ultimate appreciation he has been all these years preparing for. It is strange that it never occurred to him, when comparing himself to Noah, that if he had gone a step farther back he would have found in the ark a much closer similitude to his case, for the ark was a hundred and twenty years "a preparing," and finally saved only eight souls.

To-day is all that we can call our own; nobler work or wider spheres may never be ours, but to-day, with its appointed task, belongs to us, and the conscientious fulfillment of its duties brings a heart of peace and the Master's commendation, "Well done, thou good and faithful servant; thou hast been faithful over a few things, I will make thee ruler over many things."

Aside from those more marked qualities which we have said should characterize the recreations and the business engagements of the Christian, there are certain *minor* attributes also to be carefully cultivated. Our sterling Christian virtues will lose half their influence if they be not *courteously* exercised; our reasons for concurring in or opposing the customs of the world will fail of half their power if they be not *gently* urged; and this courtesy, this gentleness, this politeness, should belong especially to the Christian. We often find people who have apparently very faultless manners, the result of outside culture and constant friction with the world, and as we have no occasion to go beneath the surface in the casual intercourse of life, it suffices for its purpose. But when startling events come upon people and shake them out of their conventionality, no man of the world can ever be found so truly and thoroughly courteous as the man of God. His calmness, self-control and quiet care for others come from a source beyond himself; and, while the same outside opportunities for culture are open to him as to the other, the supplies of divine grace are always flowing into his soul. A rude, uncourteous Christian is a disgrace to the Church, a stumbling-block to the world and a sorrow to his Master. He may be sincere in trying to copy the inner nature of Christ, but he can have no authority for neglecting to imitate the blameless outer life which is spread out for our example. The matchless gentleness, unceasing consideration and unostentatious well-doing of our divine Master, his caressing ways to little children, his patience with ignorance, his instant forgiveness of every offence, make him a perfect model for our imperfect imitation. Can we ever forget the tender pity which made him refrain from even looking at the poor, guilty woman who was set before him, but prompted him to stoop and write upon the ground with his finger as though he saw her not, nor heard the words of her accusers?

Be assured that true Christian courtesy is a wonderful and beautiful gift; and while the sterling attributes of honor, truth and integrity prove a man's principles and piety to the world, his courtesy, gentleness and thoughtful consideration for others throw a halo around the stronger virtues which enables them to win the love as well as the respect of those about him, to conquer their hearts as well as to convince their reason. It is the mollifying oil which secures the smooth working of the wheels and cylinders of vast machinery; it is the feathered tip which carries the arrow straight to its mark.

Let our uprightness, then, be as the "iron hand" for firmness and strength; our manners as the "velvet glove" that clothes it with softness and makes its hold on others as gentle as it is strong; and our motto of action in the world the staunch old Latin maxim, used in a Christian way: "*Suaviter in modo, fortiter in re.*"

Practical Life: The Christian at Work

"*Whatsoever thy hand findeth to do, do it with thy might; for there is no work, nor device, nor knowledge, nor wisdom in the grave whither thou goest.*"—ECCLES. ix. 10.

"*I must work the works of Him that sent me, while it is day; the night cometh when no man can work.*"—JOHN ix. 4.

CHAPTER XII.

The Christian at Work.

WE can never be grateful enough to our Maker for the beneficent love he has shown in not only allowing, but in exhorting us to work for him. Prayer and praise are as sweet and refreshing to the soul as dew and sunlight; but to every active, energetic mind there is an intense delight in earnest work.

There is no portion of Christian duty which presents so many attractions at once. As a great first motive, it pleases God; it copies the example of Christ; it accomplishes good for the bodies and souls of those about us; it gratifies the naturally benevolent impulses of our heart; it gives scope to those powers within us which rejoice in action; and last, but not least important among its attributes, it reacts upon the Christian's own soul, and strengthens, develops and beautifies it in direct proportion to the efforts put forth or the sacrifices made.

It is simply impossible to do much good to others without receiving back great good to ourselves; it is like throwing a ball that rebounds, or holding up a light that shines backward as well as forward. Charity is, indeed, "twice blessed; it blesseth him that gives and him that takes;" and he that bestows good things, whether gifts of the heart, of the head, of the hands or the purse, is one of those who "scattereth, and yet increaseth;" while those who give not may withhold more than is meet, but it "tendeth to poverty."

There is, moreover, accompanying God's injunction to us to work for him a promise of success for our labors and an assurance of reward in the world to come. "He that goeth forth and weepeth, bearing precious seed, shall doubtless come again with rejoicing, bringing his sheaves with him;" and he has declared, for the encouragement of all faithful teachers and preachers, that his word, which seems so often to fall upon stony minds and into thorn-choked hearts, shall not return unto him void, but shall prosper in the thing whereto it was sent.

Ultimate success is pledged to us in this world and a full reward in the world above, but God is often better than his word, and frequently blesses us here with such an immediate and gracious return for our labors that we are repaid ten-fold, even in this life, for all that we may do in his service.

We hear a great deal about the ingratitude of the world, its grasping at favors and clamoring for more, and some clever writer has called its hollow thankfulness "a lively sense of favors to come." But every person who has been much engaged in truly useful Christian work will be able, undoubtedly, to affirm that their experience contradicts the cynical assertion. The truth is, that many people quite over-estimate the value of what they do, and require a great deal of gratitude for very minute benefits. They dwell strongly on the "cup of cold water," which our Saviour speaks of to teach us that our least labors of love are not unnoticed by him, and, having bestowed a charity as cold, as thin and as little worth to themselves, directly look for a rich return, profuse thanks and a heavenly reward.

In many cases which come to our knowledge we may rather be amazed at the amount of gratitude shown for trifling benefits, and be touched and humbled in beholding it; feeling that the poor souls must have few friends, indeed, and scanty aid for all their needs when they can afford to be so thankful for such insignificant favors.

Gratitude cannot fail to please nor ingratitude to pain us; but to let the hope of the one or the fear of the other influence our work in any way is a dishonor to the work itself. So, also, to see the immediate result of our labor is pleasing and heart-cheering; but results long delayed are no excuse for discouragement, for we know that we shall find them after many days. Higher motives and higher rewards can always be ours, and we never find the great philanthropists of the world stopping to complain of unthankfulness or of failure. If they encounter it, as they often must, it seems to produce no effect on them; they walk their lofty paths in serene patience, quite undisturbed by the praise or the censure of mortals—quite undismayed by the long-deferred fruition of their desires.

Howard, Wilberforce and Mrs. Fry worked on indefatigably because they loved their work, and we cannot imagine them giving it up in discontent for want of immediate success or for lack of human applause.

Dr. Judson, who labored so many years so faithfully in India, against untold disappointments and obstacles, has left no such feeling on record. His words upon a dying bed were, "Heaven is sweet, but I shall have all eternity to enjoy it, and I should love to work a few years longer in the vineyard of the Lord."

Eliot toiled forty years among his well-loved Indian tribes, giving time, money, study and great personal effort, with unflagging zeal and the most undaunted cheerfulness.

Brainerd, whose brief but excessive labors as a missionary at different stations resulted in sickness and early death, is said to have declared himself willing to work on for twenty years more without beholding any fruits whatever, if thereby he could encourage somebody else to occupy the field, whose more efficient labors God might bless.

We may be assured that there is a blessing not only following, but accompanying, every good work; and we may be equally certain that there is such a work for every one of us to do. God has bestowed on us a diversity of gifts, he has appointed us different lots; but in every sphere, for every soul, there is work waiting to be done. Not one of his children, however feeble or young or ignorant, may dare to say there is no work for him to accomplish.

Not long ago, in a neighboring city, there lived a woman who had once been a proficient in her trade of dress and cloak-making, but a severe illness had shattered her mind and quite unfitted her for pursuing it again. She could not endure to be idle and useless, and so would go about from house to house among the poor, to cut and fit their simple garments, always refusing to take any pay for her labors. "It is a great pleasure to me to do it," she would say in her childlike way. "God has taken away a great deal of my health and a portion of my mind; I can't go about among grand folks as I used to; I should get all confused with their rich trimmings, and make mistakes with their new patterns. I can't be trusted with so much responsibility ; it bewilders me. But I love to go from family to family among the poor, especially among God's poor. When I see the mothers worn out with over-work I like to step in and say, 'I've come to sew for you a few days.' When I know they stop going to church because their old Sunday gown isn't fit to be seen, I like just to take it and sponge it and turn it and set them going again. When I see the children staying away from Sunday-school because the weather has got cold and their shawls are thin or their cloaks worn out, it makes me happy to wad up the old cloaks again, and to fix up warm jackets to wear under the thin shawls. It's true," she would add, "God doesn't expect much of me, because he knows that my health is weakly and my mind unsettled; but when the end comes I would like to have him say, 'She hath done what she could.'"

Poor broken creature! What a living

rebuke is she to the many professing Christians who seem hardly conscious of their personal responsibility for the influence they have, or fail to have, on those about them; who seem to forget that each one of us should feel it our individual charge to leave the world, when we die, the happier and the better for our having lived in it.

The old saying, that where there is a will there is a way, was never so true of anything as of the will to serve God and benefit mankind.

A lady who was a great invalid felt much saddened at one time because it seemed as if all channels of active benevolence were closed to her. She knew her faith and love to God could find exercise in the patient endurance of the many burdens his hand had laid upon her, but she longed to do something for the bodies or souls of her fellowmen. She resolved to watch for every opportunity of well-doing, and prayed God to open her eyes to see whatever such he might send, for she determined if it were possible that even she, invalid as she was, would do at least one kind or useful thing for others each day.

She kept a little calendar to satisfy her own mind and to test the possibility of carrying out her plan, and its record was really surprising.

For weeks and months together there were but a few days without the "golden deed" to crown them, and those were times of great sickness. Often it was nothing more than sending a bowl of broth or a plate of fruit to a sick person; sometimes it was only enclosing a little tract or hymn to some one at a distance with a few kind words; once it was interceding for a penitent boy who had lost a good place through misconduct.

With great care she selected a small library of the best and most interesting religious books she could find, and loaned them to servants and poor people; and then, too sick to teach in Sunday-school, she gathered in a class of ignorant children who worked all day in the factory and came to her in the evening to be taught. Through the children she was enabled to reach the parents, and sometimes to render them material assistance, so that the usefulness which she feared was denied her spread and spread till it embraced a sphere almost too large for one heart and one pair of hands to minister to.

It is said that Dr. Arnold's sister, who was an invalid for twenty years, was the very sunshine of the household. Her sick room was the haven where every one came for rest, for sympathy and for cheerful encouragement.

If those whom God afflicts with bodily pain and weakness can accomplish so much for his service and the happiness of others, how much more may well be expected of those who have health and youth and every faculty of mind and body!

The field is wide, the work is great, the harvest ripe and the laborers few. No Christian, bearing as he does the name of Christ, should be satisfied with himself unless he is engaged in some good work for the Master. If one kind is not at hand, another is; if one sort is not fitted to his powers, another will exactly suit him. It is only absurd to say we cannot do this or that, until we have tried, and tried faithfully. We can never tell the riches of a mine till we work it, neither can we tell what powers may be developed in our minds and characters when they come face to face with the work before us. If we cannot do it as well as somebody else might, let us, at least, do the best we can, and until that better one arrives seek, in all the service that we offer our Master, to merit the all-sufficient commendation, "She hath done what she could."

We are all of us doing an unconscious work, whether we will or not—a work that we cannot cease from if we would—the work of silent, involuntary influence. As noiseless as the falling dew, as the rising of the sun, as the setting of the tides, but as uninterrupted as they in its constant action, its constant influence upon others. It is the result of being good more than of doing good, it is the effect of righteousness at rest instead of in motion.

Two ladies met in a friend's house not long ago; twenty-five years before they had passed a few weeks together, and had never met since.

"I have often wanted to see you," said one of them to the other, "for I owe you a great deal. I consider that you were the means of my becoming a Christian. You changed the whole course of my life, under God, in those few weeks we spent together long ago."

"I can hardly believe it possible," the other replied in astonishment; "I was scarcely more than a girl, and I do not remember ever talking with you on religious subjects."

"You never did, directly," returned her friend; "but your whole life was a lovely, pure, faithful, Christian life. It won me, and impressed me irresistibly. You were, indeed, scarcely more than a girl, but you proved to me how doubly winning even fresh, bright youth can be, when sanctified by God's spirit; you showed me the beauty of holiness, and I owe to you the influences that brought me to Christ."

Thus we see that simply by being good we are producing a powerful, though involuntary effect upon others; but the conscientious Christian will not be satisfied to rest there. In fact, it is almost invariably found that those persons who are the most consistent in the more passive phases of Christian life are also most faithful in its active duties.

But how many are there among professing Christians who are actually doing all or a half or even a small portion of what they might do? Alas! only a handful, a feeble band, a scattered few, compared with the thousands who call themselves members of the Church of Christ and are pledged to do its work and to fight its battles.

If these multitudes of dormant Christians only knew the happiness, the blessedness, of the Master's work, they would engage in it for their own sakes. If they only considered the awful, pressing needs of their fellow-creatures, they would pursue it for the world's sake. If they would but remember the words of the Saviour and his moving example, they would consecrate themselves to it for Christ's sake.

There has been an estimate made with regard to individual Christian work in the conversion of the world which gives a startling result. "If each one," says a recent religious writer, "by proper effort, with God's blessing, should secure the conversion of one soul within the year, then there would be an army of twenty millions of workmen instead of the ten only now in the vineyard; and if we could go forward another year in the same manner, then there would be forty millions of Christians instead of twenty; the next year eighty millions; the next one hundred and sixty; and at that rate the whole world would be converted to Christ in seven years."

Upon whom rests this immense responsibility? Who is to blame if these possible conversions do not take place? Clearly, each and every Christian who is failing to fulfill his part in active effort for the salvation of souls.

By their fruits, it is said, ye shall know them; and if, in despite of the mighty motives which combine to impel us irresistibly to the most earnest and unceasing endeavor, we remain cold, indifferent or idle, the inference is almost inevitable that our religion is but an outside form, that our hearts have never been breathed upon by the Holy

Spirit, nor warmed by the fervent love of Christ—that we have, in fact, like the Church at Sardis, a name that we live, and are dead.

"Behold, these three years," said the master of the vineyard, "I come seeking fruit on this fig tree and find none. Cut it down; why cumbereth it the ground?" Like Israel, we are but an empty vine; like the fruitless fig tree, we offer for the husbandman's inspection nothing but leaves.

> "And shall we meet the Master so,
> Bearing our withered leaves?
> The Saviour is looking for perfect fruit.
> Stand we before him, sad and mute,
> Waiting the word he breathes,
> 'Nothing but leaves!'"

May God in his mercy forbid such a fate to any who bear the name of Christ! The power that turned us from death unto life can enable us to make that life a heartfelt offering to the Redeemer of the world. By the capacity for growth that he has implanted in our souls; by the standard of attainment he has placed before us; by the spiritual influences to be found in prayer and praise, in open worship or in secret study of his word; by the winning beauty of those fruits he has bidden us bring forth; at home, abroad, in sickness or health, in grief or gladness,—may we be inspired, impelled, to go forward from grace to grace, from strength to. strength, doing his whole will.

Let us work the works of Him that has sent us while it is day, for the night cometh when no man can work; the night of death to mortal bodies—the night of eternal gloom to immortal souls unreconciled to God.

What mighty deeas could we not accomplish in our united strength if every one who is called by the name of Christ were but a faithful, working Christian! We should go forth as an invincible host, an irresistible phalanx of conquerors; we should speedily possess the whole world, and the Church would become what Solomon said of her as the Bride of the Lamb, "Fair as the moon, clear as the sun and terrible as an army with banners." The prince of this world would be dethroned, the King of saints established for ever, his peaceful sceptre have perfect sway, and the Church Militant give place to the Church Triumphant.

THE END.

www.ingramcontent.com/pod-product-compliance
Lightning Source LLC
LaVergne TN
LVHW011209110826
845150LV00006B/1376

* 9 7 8 1 4 2 5 5 1 7 8 2 3 *